NAVIGATING LIFE

A Father's Life Lessons for His Children

DOUGLAS
POOLE

Navigating Life: A Father's Life Lessons for His Children /
Douglas Poole

ISBN: 978-0-615-52664-5

Printed and bound in the United States of America

Cover Image: ©iStockphoto/Monika Lewandowska

This book is dedicated to the love of my life
and my soul's mate, Jacqueline Bishop Poole,
and to the pride and joy of my life:
Sarah, Jonathan, Michael, and Bethany.

ACKNOWLEDGMENTS

My heart is full of immeasurable appreciation for my family of origin: Don and Lucille Poole are more than anyone could ask for in parents and much of what is written here is based on the principles I learned from them and their example. My "Little Sister" Cyndi makes being a brother one of the best assignments a guy could ever have.

Thanks goes to a gang of guys who have moved in and out of my life during different seasons, but who have all contributed to making me both want to and actually be a better husband, father, leader, and man: Ron Wiegert (my cousin and only cradle-to-grave friend), Tim Dunagan, Lavern Krull, Dave "Latto" Larson, Randy Discher, Denny Huebner, Dickie Callahan, Alan Schellenbach, Steve Meyers, Arlan Larson, Scott Kelby (who believed I had something to offer worth putting into print and then got in my face and challenged me to put pen to paper), Russell Moir, Gary Buchanan, Caleb Deliard, and my partner in prayer, Art Dunfee.

Thanks, as well, to a group of women who have been "spiritual sisters" determined to keep this "brother" in line: Aunt Florence Krull, Mom Carol Davis, Patsy Brown, Lori Meyers, Alana Stephenson, Kalebra Kelby, Connie Buchanan, Molly Bail, Grandma Mary Joos, Grandma Faye Thomson, and Cheryl Khan.

And, of course, my gratitude to Cypress Meadows Community Church (one of the best churches on the planet) couldn't be greater. Together, we have built a community of faith, hope, and love that is infusing Gods grace deep into our own lives and with a reach wide enough to join hands with our partners in Haiti and Kenya. Faithful elders and spiritual leaders like Paul Steinbrueck, Jim Gregorich, and Donna Chamberlain have kept me and Cypress on track and lead us in a prevailing way.

Then there is Kim Doty (editor extraordinaire), who really understood the depth of what was in my heart for my children when I wrote this book and she then made it her personal mission to help me create something worthy of my heart's passion.

Finally, and most importantly, I want to thank God who thought a wretch like me was worth loving and giving of the life of His one and only son Jesus Christ. I will never recover (nor do I want to) from the wonder of the grace He has bestowed on me. I am so aware that I get to lead an over-privileged life and my hope is that my life is lived as an expression of my unending gratitude to my Father above. His grace is nothing but amazing. It has rescued me, directed me, provided for me, healed me, sustained me, and will one day come back for me. And ten thousand years from now, when every other word has been worn out and used up, I expect to just be getting warmed up in my appreciation for His grace. I serve a wonderful...wonderful...wonderful God!

TABLE OF CONTENTS

PRELUDE

Sarah, Jonathan, Michael, and Bethany:

As soon as you were born and I could pry you out of the doctor's hands, I swept you up in my arms, drew you close, and whispered the first words you heard into your ear. Three short phrases: "[Your name]…I love you… Jesus Christ is Lord." I wanted you to know your identity, your value, and your Lord from your first breath of air.

From the moment I laid eyes on you, my heart confirmed what it felt that day Mom said you were growing inside her…captured, totally captured, and I was hopelessly, irretrievably head over heels in love with you. You are the best gifts any dad could ever ask for and I often find myself marveling at how privileged I am to have you kids and your mom in my life. And I will keep marveling over this till I draw my last breath.

The hope and dream Mom and I have for you is that you know and experience the fullness of life God created you for. You see, when your love for someone is so intense and immense that it blows the lid off every and any chart or scale you use to try and measure it…you just can't help but want that person to fully know and fully experience the life God has for them—a life of purpose, satisfaction, and success in every realm.

This kind of life is not dependent so much upon where you are in respect to location or age. This kind of life is not dependent so much upon what you have in respect to possessions or position in life. Rather fully experiencing the life your heart longs for is primarily a function of who you are, what you know, and what you do.

I have lived long enough and had a front row seat in enough peoples' lives to say with a high degree of confidence that you can be full of possessions and positions of power and still have an empty life. You can have a 3-karat diamond on your left ring finger and still have an empty marriage. You can have closets full of clothes, calendars full of appointments, bank accounts full of money, houses full of prime square footage, a body full of beauty and strength, and still be living an unfulfilled, empty, and bankrupt life. Ultimately, a rewarding and fulfilling life is something much different than that. So I write this in an effort to help you navigate the journey only you can take…the adventure of life. A life that both your heavenly Father and your earthly father hope you live to its fullest.

All my love—Dad

PART I

Sailing Essentials

Choosing to Sail

"Twenty years from now you will be more disappointed
by the things that you didn't do than by the ones you did do.
So throw off the bowlines. Sail away from the safe harbor.
Catch the trade winds in your sails. Explore. Dream. Discover."

—MARK TWAIN

This is your life. This is your one and only life. Question: What are you doing with your one and only life?

I knew a man once who was bright, witty, and full of so much potential it made others envious. When he was young, people said of him, "He will do something with his life." Then somewhere in his early adult years it became obvious that he was underachieving for someone with so much potential. And so people around him began to say, "He could do something if he just applied himself." The years passed and now people say of him, "He could have done something if he had just tried." His life is a tragic story of unfulfilled potential and unrealized dreams. A story of a life squandered away; a story of settling for less. A story of would have, could have, should have. Don't let his story be your story! For heaven's sake, don't let this be your story.

Let me say it again. This is your life, your one and only life. What are you doing with your one and only life? What you are living today is not the prelude to your life, this is your life. Your life doesn't begin at graduation, when you get married, land a job, have a child, own a home, or turn 20,

30, or 40 for that matter. Your life began as a creation of God's grace and your parents' love. The life you have lived, up to today, has helped shape and determine the life you are experiencing right now, but it does not have to determine your tomorrows. Yesterday has come and gone. What has happened, happened. You can't change or undo yesterday, it is what it is. Learn from and leverage both the good and bad of yesterday, but don't try to live in it. Yesterday is a memory. You can't seize today or move into tomorrow when you are living in yesterday.

Today is a new day and a day that will greatly influence your tomorrows. You see, the life you are living today is a series of moments that you either seize or let sift through your fingers. Today is all you have; you have no guarantees of tomorrow. So you must learn to seize the opportunities, the moments called "today."

The life you will live tomorrow is influenced and shaped by how you choose to seize your moments today. So choose wisely. And remember, you only get one shot at this life. One shot, that's it…so make it your best shot. This is no dress rehearsal, this is the show. So seize the day, everyday, because days have a way of turning into weeks, weeks into months, months into years, and years into a lifetime. This is your one and only life. What are you doing with your one and only life? You don't want to get to the end of your life, and look back on a mountain of regrets from opportunities missed and moments un-seized. You want your life to matter. You want to live boldly, love deeply, dream greatly, and execute wisely. What are you doing with your one and only life today? What will you be doing with your one and only life tomorrow? Are you lying at anchor in the bay of yesterday and letting life pass you by? Will you drift through your today, moving along with the tides of the times, the currents of culture, and the wind of whatever comes your way? Or will you take responsibility for your one and only life, seizing your moments today as you sail into your preferred future? Which will it be? It's your life, you get to decide. But choose wisely.

Oh, and if not now, then when, in which lifetime, will you make the wise choice? It's never too late to start. Remember, yesterday has shaped and influenced your today. But yesterday doesn't have to determine your tomorrows. So sail, my child, sail, dream, and risk.

My prayer for you is the prayer of an ancient sailor who dreamed big, took a calculated risk, and sailed around the world in 1577. His name was Sir Francis Drake and this is his prayer:

> *Disturb us, Lord, when*
> *We are too well pleased with ourselves,*
> *When our dreams have come true*
> *Because we have dreamed too little,*
> *When we arrived safely*
> *Because we sailed too close to the shore.*
>
> *Disturb us, Lord, when*
> *With the abundance of things we possess*
> *We have lost our thirst*
> *For the waters of life;*
> *Having fallen in love with life,*
> *We have ceased to dream of eternity*
> *And in our efforts to build a new earth,*
> *We have allowed our vision*
> *Of the new heaven to dim.*
>
> *Disturb us, Lord, to dare more boldly,*
> *To venture on the wider seas*
> *Where storms will show your mastery;*
> *Where losing sight of land*
> *We shall find the stars.*
>
> *We ask You to push back*
> *The horizons of our hopes;*
> *And to push into the future*
> *In strength, courage, hope, and love.*
>
> *This we ask in the name of our Captain,*
> *Who is Jesus Christ.*

- 2 -

The Call of the Sea

"I must go down to the seas again,
for the call of the running tide
is a wild call and a clear call
that may not be denied;..."

—JOHN EDWARD MASEFIELD, FROM "SEA FEVER"

O nce you choose to sail, once you decide you want your one and only life to matter, that you want to experience a full life that reaches full potential, you must then begin to figure out *where* you want to sail, right?! A sail to no where on a Sunday afternoon in Tampa Bay can make for a pleasant outing. A sail to nowhere with your life is an entirely different story. A story that takes you to a land of missed opportunities, with a mountain of regrets.

I remember your mom and I once taking what we thought was going to be a little romantic sail to nowhere, on a certain February 14th. A sail we now fondly remember as the "St. Valentine's Day Disaster." We had just purchased our first sailboat in January and even though my captaining experience was limited to all of less than 30 days, I was not about to let a little detail like that, nor the 18 plus-knot winds that were blowing, keep me from giving my first mate the kind of romantic day on the water I wanted and she deserved.

As Mom drove to work that morning, she was met by a series of signs I had strategically posted on telephone poles along the way inviting her to the sail of her life with the man of her dreams. After school that day, I whisked her off to the boat and out into the bay which was teeming with whitecaps. I was such a novice at the time—I didn't even know the basic drill of reefing the mainsail to reduce the sail size in higher winds. So, I soon found myself overpowered and I found your mom in a white-knuckled panic as we heeled enough to put the rail dangerously close to the water. Since I in no way wanted to feed into your mom's near panic, I kept on my game face to give the appearance that all was under control, but inside I was shooting, "Help me, Jesus!" flare prayers toward heaven! It quickly became apparent that this romantic sail was not going to leave Mom in an amorous mood. So, I decided to fire up the "iron ginny," drop sail and motor in, only to discover that the flywheel was locked up. (I didn't know it at the time, but with that motor, if you pulled the kill cord with the motor in gear, you had to take the top off and tinker with the gear cable in order to restart the engine.) Now, here we were with too much sail for a novice and no motor to come to my rescue. I kept my game face on and assured Mom…"No problem."

Now, I am silently shooting up more flare prayers and trying to figure out how to solve my "no problem" problem and get us safely back to the dock. However, due to other boat traffic, an outgoing tide, and wind direction, my first pass at the dock was a clean miss. No problem, a quick tack and we'll do take two, or so I thought. The tack took me out of the channel, the centerboard got caught up, and we got stuck in irons. No problem, I'll just backfill the main and get us out. Instead, we drifted up on the mud flats and really got stuck. (In case you were wondering, any romantic sparkle left in Mom's eyes was now gone. In fact, if I remember right, and I'm sure I do, the sparkle had been replaced by daggers.)

Did I mention it was February? As you know, February nights can be a bit chilly. As the sun set, the wind totally died, so we lost our only source of power to return to the dock. And, yes, the temperature did begin to plummet. Oh, and did I mention we had no food, no blankets, and no lights. No problem, I figured I'd just call out to any passing boaters as I tried to reach someone on the cell phone. Boaters were a little scarce on the water that night (I wonder why?). All I could do was leave voice mails with a friend or two. No problem, I'll just jump in and push us off the mud flats. Unfortunately, the water was deeper than I thought, colder than I anticipated, the bottom muckier than I realized, and the plan less effective than I had hoped. Now, I'm wet and cold—never a very good combination. No problem, I'll just shoot more flare prayers toward heaven. It was about then, along came a fisherman in his skiff. Yea, God! We flagged him down. He was sympathetic to our plight, gave us a tow, and sometime after dark-thirty we were back to the dock. Oh, and in case you were wondering, which I am sure you are, the feel of land under your mom's feet did not return the Valentine's Day sparkle into her eyes. It's a wonder she ever went back out on the water with me again.

Now, imagine standing on a dock talking with a sailor who is casting off dock lines and is preparing to set sail. You ask, "Where are you sailing to?" His response, "I don't know." So you ask, "How will you know when you get there?" Again, the sailor responds, "I don't know." You press on, "How long will you be out to sea?" Again, he replies, "I don't know." You inquire, "Do you have enough gear, sails, and provisions?" Once more you hear that predictable answer, "I don't know."

You venture two more questions, "Is your boat sea worthy? Will it withstand the inevitable storms and rough seas that will come your way?" "I don't know" is the sailor's final reply.

Anybody want to set sail on that boat? No destination, no time frames, no provisions…no thanks.

Such a sail may sound a little adventurous and maybe a little romantic at first. However, believe me, all it will take is one of life's storms, a breakdown, a shortage, or a few days of being lost at sea to convince you otherwise.

Nevertheless, it never ceases to amaze me the number of people who would never, ever consider boarding a boat for a sail of that nature, yet they set sail with their one and only life in such a fashion…drifting aimlessly here and there, landing at the same dead end port over and over. Or they are always falling short of what could have and should have been. Is that really the life you want? Like I said, no thanks!

So how do you go about making that huge, life-altering decision of figuring out where you are going to sail with your one and only life? If you want to lead a rich and rewarding life, one that reaches full potential…well then getting this right is pretty important, wouldn't you say? Of course, it is.

Sailors of old would speak of the "call of the sea"—that mysterious, compelling, driving force that kept pulling them to get back on board, and heading out to sea for another voyage. The deal is, a true sailor is never totally and completely at home on dry land. Visiting new ports can be exciting, spending time with landlubbers can be meaningful, and shore leave is welcomed, but as good as land life can be it has a shelf life for a true sailor. The day comes when a restlessness begins to build, a desire to breathe in salt air grows, the yearning for the sound of the waves washing against the hull of the vessel, and a longing for the motion of the boat moving across the open water. The sailor says, "The sea is calling me. There is salt water running through my veins. I've got to get out to sea or I'll go nuts here on land." In the words of that renowned cartoon sailor, Popeye, "That's all I can stand, I can't stands no more!" Get me back out to sea!

True sailors are only fully alive when they are out to sea, doing what they were made to do. And that is exactly what you want to discover for your one and only life. What is the "call of the sea" for you? What were you made to do? What is that compelling call, that driving force for you? Figure that out and you will know where your journey will take you. The question, of course, is how to go about figuring this out.

Well, I've discovered it's part art and part science. There are some things you can do and some voices you can listen to that will help guide you in determining where you will sail to with your one and only life. Those voices are:

+ The voice of God
+ The voice of your heart
+ The voice of experience
+ The voice of your strengths
+ The voice of wise people
+ The voice of your gut

The Voice of God

For too many years of my life, in my younger days, I lived with the mistaken notion that if I really looked to God for direction in my life, He'd take me somewhere I didn't want to go; have me do things I really didn't enjoy and I wasn't very good at. And worse, stick me with people I didn't really want to be with. Nothing could be further from the truth.

Instead, one of the things that makes life such a rewarding and fulfilling adventure for me is listening to and following the voice of God. Both Scripture and life experience say we have a God in heaven who is head over heels in love with us. He created us in His image so that we might enjoy the deepest levels of soul-satisfying community with Him while fulfilling His purpose for our lives. When God created us, He hard-wired into us certain aptitudes, abilities, desires, and passions. And when we discover who God uniquely made us to be, as well as the unique gifts and strengths He designed for us, it leads to a remarkably fulfilling and fruitful life. What's more, Scripture says, God delights in revealing that information to us.

So, if you want to figure out what your life journey will be about, doesn't it just make sense to go to the One who loves you more than you could ever know, holds your best interest at heart, knows what is going to bring purpose and fulfillment to you, says His plans are to prosper you and give you hope and a future, and promises to lead you down that path if you will trust Him with all your heart, lean not on your understanding but in all your ways acknowledge Him?

How do you listen for the voice of God? For starters, just pray. Tell God you want to figure the best direction to head with your life, acknowledging that He knows you better than you know yourself. He holds your best interest at heart. He knows the purpose for which you were created. Ask *Him* to guide you down that path.

Will you hear an audible voice? The overwhelming odds are, *no*. Will you have a vision in the middle of the night? Most likely not. Will there be a cloud formation that spells it out? Don't spend your days staring at the sky for that. Instead, listen carefully for the voice of God to lead you in a chorus of the following voices.

The Voice of Your Heart

The heart speaks to us through our passions, longings, and desires. The heart answers the question, "If I could do anything in the world and I knew I wouldn't fail, what would I do?" Find a place to ruminate on that question; a quiet place. A place where you will be undisturbed, a place away from all the exterior noise, and a place where you can lower the internal noise of all the voices in your head that are screaming for attention. Just be still and ask yourself, "What is in my heart to do with my one and only life?" What would I do if I could do anything in this life and know I wouldn't fail?

Most often it takes awhile to quiet both the external and internal noise enough to hear the voice of your heart and it might even take a few attempts. But if you really give yourself to listening, your heart will speak to you. What do you long to do? What makes your heart beat fast?

The Voice of Experience

Somewhere in the course of your life up to this point, I really hope you have been engaged in some activity where you felt fully alive. So alive and so meaningful that time seemed to fly by. You realized that not only did you enjoy what you were doing, but you were actually sort of good at it. Maybe really good, and you couldn't wait to do this again. Can you think of moments like that in your life?

Odds are you can probably also remember some experiences that were the polar opposite. Activities or events that you found no pleasure in, nothing seemed to call out the best in you, the thing seemed to drag on forever, it felt like something inside you was dying and you dreaded the thought of facing that drill again. No doubt, you can think of moments like that, as well.

And I'm sure you've got plenty of experiences that were somewhat of a mixed bag, not all great, but not all that bad either.

When it comes to deciding where to sail with your one and only life, which sounds better: doing something you're not all that good at and it fills you with dread or doing something you not only enjoy, but that you are half-way good at?

Listen to the experiences of your life. They will help to guide you. Experiment a little. Try a few safe, low-risk deals. Then ask yourself, "Did I enjoy it? Am I or could I be adept at this with a little training? Could I see myself doing this day in, day out?"

What do you truly have the potential to be really good at, what do you really enjoy?

The Voice of Your Strengths

The following story is from the *Springfield, Oregon, Public Schools Newsletter*:

Once upon a time, the animals decided they should do something meaningful to meet the problems of the new world. So they organized a school.

They adopted an activity curriculum of running, climbing, swimming, and flying. To make it easier to administer the curriculum, all the animals took all the subjects.

The *duck* was excellent at swimming; in fact, better than his instructor. But he made only passing grades in flying, and was very poor at running. Since he was slow in running, he had to drop swimming and stay after school to practice running. This caused his web feet to be badly worn, so that he was only average in swimming. But average was quite acceptable, so nobody worried about that—except the duck.

The *rabbit* started at the top of his class in running, but developed a nervous twitch in his leg muscles because of so much make-up work in swimming.

The *squirrel* was excellent in climbing, but he encountered constant frustration in flying class because his teacher made him start from the ground up, instead of from the treetop down. He developed "charlie horses" from overexertion, and so he only got a C in climbing and a D in running.

The *eagle* was a problem child and was severely disciplined for being a non-conformist. In climbing, he beat all the others to the top of the tree, but insisted on using his way to get there.

A duck is a duck—and *only* a duck. It is built to swim, not to run or fly and certainly not to climb. A squirrel is a squirrel—and *only* that. To move it out of its forte, climbing, and then expect it to swim or fly will drive a squirrel nuts. Eagles are beautiful creatures in the air, but not in a foot race. The rabbit will win every time unless, of course, the eagle gets hungry.

What is true of creatures in the forest is true of people. God has not made us all the same. He never intended to. It was He who planned and designed the differences and unique strengths.

If God made you a duck—you're a duck. Swim like mad, but don't get bent out of shape because you wobble when you run or flap instead of fly. Furthermore, if you're an eagle, stop expecting squirrels to soar, or rabbits to build the same kind of nests you do.

So relax. Enjoy your strengths. Cultivate your own capabilities; your own style. Appreciate others for who they are, even though their outlook or style may be miles different from yours. Rabbits don't fly. Eagles don't swim. Ducks look funny trying to climb. Squirrels don't have feathers.

The career training I received had in it a sort of "weakness resolution" mentality. I was basically told that in order to have a strong and successful career, I needed to focus my energy, attention, and efforts on "fixing" my weaknesses. I've come to see that line of thinking as being wrong, just plain wrong.

You see, God seems to have hard-wired into us all a set of strengths. Areas where we just seem to naturally do well, if not excel. Likewise, we all have areas where certain other people just seem to naturally be stronger, more adept, and way more easily accomplished than we are. It is what it is.

Here's also what I noticed: When I focused on improving my weaknesses, it took enormous energy to achieve only incremental improvement. The whole process drained the life out of me. Conversely, when I focused on developing my strengths, it seemed to take less energy, I got way better results, and it poured life into me. Hmmm. So, I decided it was a much better investment to pour into areas where I am naturally drawn and good at, thereby experiencing a measure of greatness. This was a way better investment than pouring into areas of weaknesses where, at best, I could hope to be mediocre.

I made the decision that unless a weakness is a fatal flaw that would do me in, I wouldn't address it. So, put 90–95% of your attention on your strengths and 5–10% on your weaknesses. You will be most successful by building your life around your strengths than around your weaknesses. So, pick up a good strengths-finding assessment tool, take it, then by all means live it.

The Voice of Wise People

Look around at the people in your relational world. Who is it that others seem to look to for counsel? Who do others lean into for advice? Who seems to be able to discern what is really going on when others are a little confused? Who usually seems to end up on the right side of things? Who will tell you what you really need to hear, even if it's not what you really want to hear? Got anybody like that in your life?

People like that are far and few between and I've always made it my business to ensure that I have a small but powerful "personal board of directors" in my life. Wise, truth-speaking people who I know care about what happens in my life. Get up next to a handful of people who love you, then humbly and openly ask them what they could see you doing with the rest of your life. Don't be surprised if the questions they ask far out number the advice they offer. The really wise often want to help you learn to lead your life wisely more than they want to lead your life for you.

These wise people may be a leader in your church, a grandparent, a respected family friend, a teacher, or who knows maybe even a parent. But find someone who does life well, then ask and listen.

The Voice of Your Gut

Inside you somewhere is a "gut meter" and your gut meter tells you what really matters and what really doesn't. If your gut says, "Sorry, but can you really see yourself doing this for the rest of your life?" Or "Is this really worthy of you getting up, going into work, doing this day in day out for the next 30 years?" Or if you just get a "gut check" and can't pinpoint why, it's worth listening to and finding out what is causing it. Is it just the pizza you ate last night that didn't settle well or is it a career choice that you couldn't stomach for long? Learn to listen to your gut.

I've lived to regret ignoring a few gut checks in my life. Likewise, sometimes your gut will say, "Go for it!" Does that mean you should ignore common sense and blindly take off? No. But it does mean you should find out why your gut is giving you a green light.

17

The voice of God, the voice of your heart, the voice of experience, the voice of your strengths, the voice of wise people, and the voice of your gut—put them together and given time and intentionality, you will hear your "call of the sea." You will know where you are going to sail with your one and only life.

Maybe it will be to lead a company. Maybe it will be to teach at a school or university. Maybe it will be in sales, medicine, agriculture, or the church. Are you a leader, a builder, an entrepreneur, an engineer, a designer, a writer, or a problem-solver?

Where will you sail to with your one and only life?

Captain's Log

The "call of the sea" for me resulted in a four-fold purpose for my life. After carefully listening to the "voices," I found a quiet place where I could sit down with my journal, reflect, and pray. Sometime later, I wrote these words: My life will be about...

1. Being a fully devoted follower of Jesus Christ.
2. Having a fully connected marriage.
3. Being a fully engaged father.
4. Being a full-potential leader of Cypress Meadows
   Community Church.

I then wrote out a life plan, complete with a strategy of activities I would do, books I would read, actions steps I would take that were written in ink on my planner. Every year, I review, tweak, or change the plan to ensure I really am about what I say I am about.

- 3 -

Finding Your North Star

"When your values are clear to you,
making decisions becomes easier."

—ROY DISNEY, WORLD-CLASS SAILOR

S ailors of old crossed the vast expanses of open sea in uncharted waters where there were no landmarks by relying on the one constant in their world at sea…Polaris, the North Star. Using a sextant by day and celestial navigation by night, sailors could determine their geographical position and plot their course. By knowing where Polaris was, sailors could recalibrate after a storm knocked them off course a few degrees. A sailor's very life on the open sea rested on the ability to find the North Star for navigation.

No one in their right mind wants to aimlessly meander around in open water "hoping" that they are headed on the right coordinates. Nor do you want to go through life "hoping" that you are headed in the right direction with your career, your marriage, your parenting, your finances, or anything else in your life. Without a North Star, how will you know if your finances are on course? Without a relational Polaris to help you navigate, how will you get your marriage back on the right path after a relational storm? What will you use to recalibrate when your parenting gets off a few degrees.

If you don't know these things, the day will come when you will wonder:

"How in the world did my career ever end up here?"

"What happened to our marriage…we started out so good, how did we end up so disconnected and so far apart?"

"How did the dreams I once had for my life, ever go so far astray?"

What is your North Star that you will use to navigate toward the life your heart longs for? What will be the constants in your life that are non-negotiable? Constants are those beliefs that keep you from going astray, on course, and headed toward the right destination. Values are the constants that serve as the North Star to guide you as you navigate through life. Values not only help you to chart the right course to sail, they also keep you on track and out of trouble. Values warn you of shoals, mud flats, and reefs. History is full of stories of men and women who violated basic values in life and shipwrecked their marriage on a reef; ran their career or finances aground; or just plain sailed around in circles all their life. Don't number yourself among these people.

In the end, you must decide which values will serve as your North Star to chart the course by which you will sail. Will you value truth-speaking or deceit? Integrity or duplicity? Hard work or apathy? What are your core values? Determine them wisely for they will shape your decision making; be reflected in your spending; be the gate keeper for what gets on your calendar; and will be a filter for who you let get closest to you.

One of my personal values is that I value fulfilling the bidding of God's will in my life. After going through a somewhat long and at times arduous process of determining what God wanted me to do with my life (lead Cypress Meadows Community Church), it made other decisions quite easy for me. So, when I was asked to relocate our family to places like Nebraska, Minnesota, Alabama, New Jersey, other cities in Florida, or places like Australia and New Zealand…no sweating, no agonizing, just a polite "No thanks." And when I was asked to create and head up a new department in a college, it was flattering but it wasn't inviting. And when I was asked to lead a company for a friend, again I had a North Star to navigate by; the value of doing God's bidding, which for me was to lead Cypress Meadows to be a prevailing church.

The good news is you don't have to just settle for taking a blind stab at which values to adhere to. History is also full of accounts of those who have successfully sailed before us. Their lives and stories leave a legacy of values that have been tried, tested, and proven trustworthy for millenniums. Not days, weeks, months, decades, nor centuries, but for millenniums.

Captain's Log

I was challenged once to figure out my personal core values and then to intentionally live according to them. I took the challenge to heart one day and created this list:

1. I value leading a fully devoted, authentic Christ-like life.

2. I value oneness in marriage.

3. I value raising whole, well-adjusted Christ-following children.

4. I value being a contributing part of a loving biblical community.

5. I value fulfilling the bidding of God's will in my life.

6. I value financial freedom.

7. I value engaging in God-honoring recreation.

8. I value being in physical shape.

9. I value mentoring the next generation of Christian leaders.

- 4 -

Plotting Your Course

"I can't change the direction of the wind,

but I can adjust my sails

to always reach my destination."

—JIMMY DEAN

I t was a beautiful Florida winter day. Sunshine, blue skies, temperature in the low 70's, and the prevailing south-easterlies were blowing at about 10 knots. A near perfect day for a sail. And to make the day complete, it was Dr. Martin Luther King, Jr. Day, which meant no work, no school…no excuses to not take advantage of this gorgeous day and sail.

I knew where we would sail—to the Bahama Breeze restaurant. I had a chart of upper Tampa Bay to serve as my "North Star," which would keep me off the mud flats and guide me through the channels, and by now I'd had enough experience under my belt to avoid another St. Valentine's Day disaster. What I didn't have was a course plotted to get us there. Sort of an important dimension of making the day an enjoyable one, wouldn't you say? Having never been there by water before, I had no idea which channel to take in order to navigate our way through the rat's maze of waterways that stood between the marina and the restaurant.

Rather than just taking off and "trusting my gut" or finding it by trial and error, thus increasing the risk of mutiny by the soon-to-be starving and impatient crew of family on board, the better part of wisdom said to plot a course before pulling out of the boat slip. So, I got out the charts, plotted a course, and consulted with a few of the "old salts" in the marina who had made this day sail before. They gave me some insights from their experience regarding some nuances that weren't on the chart and some advice on how to best approach the restaurant docks on a changing tide.

It was great weather, a great sail, great food, and great company which all made for a great day.

When you know where you want to go, and you know how to get there, it not only helps make for a great sail, it can make for a great life. In my life, I've met so many (way too many) people who thought they knew what they wanted in life—things like financial freedom, a rewarding career, a soul-connected marriage, a fulfilling spiritual life, and to be in good physical shape. Great destinations, yet often when I sat down with these people and asked them how they were going to get there, most often I discovered they had no real, true course they were intentionally following to get there. Then they wondered why they kept going aground financially; why they kept ending up at the wrong career destination; why they kept drifting relationally; or back at the same old place with their physical condition.

If you can't spell out how you are going to get somewhere, odds are you'll never make it. Good intentions are good, but good intentions alone never got anyone to a great destination. No one drifts into a loving and connected marriage. People don't accidentally stumble into financial freedom. And rewarding careers are not the result of just going with the flow.

How do you want to go through life? Drifting with the current and shifting winds, wandering about aimlessly? Or do you want to intentionally head somewhere with a clear plan by which you know you are on course and going to where you want to go. The answer is obvious isn't it?

So let's talk about the course-plotting loop. The elements of the loop are: plan, execute, review, and revise. Course plotting in life is a loop because life is an ongoing journey and the natural gravitational pull always seems to go south if left alone. Think about it. Stop working your health plan, stop working out, or stop following a good eating plan, and what direction will things head? Will you naturally become stronger, shapelier, and sleeker? Or will things head in the other direction? Stop investing in a relationship, cease communicating, give up on problem solving, and will that relationship improve and deepen? Or will distance and frustration develop? Stop working a financial plan, stop adhering to solid, proven financial management, and what happens? You get the idea. Course plotting is a continual loop of planning, executing, reviewing the progress, revising the plan, and then executing all over again.

Plan

A good plan is derived by four phases: gathering information, assessing options, selecting a plan, and creating action steps with timelines.

Phase 1: Gather Information

The wise sage, Solomon, once said, "There is nothing new under the sun." That certainly applies here. There is a literal gold mine of insight available to you in Scripture, the writings of experts, and the experience of others. Most often there is no need to reinvent or just blindly take a stab at something. So educate yourself. Dig around in the wisdom of Scripture and learn the elements of what makes for great relationships. Go to the bookstore and pick up a copy of a good book on financial management.

Sit down with someone further ahead of you on the career path and pick their brain. Get up next to people whose lives you respect and consult with them. Learn from both their successes and their failures. Humble yourself, ask, listen carefully and respectfully. Summarize what you heard them say, then ask if you heard it correctly. Express your appreciation for their time and counsel, then take what you can use and leave the rest.

Phase 2: Assess Your Options

Gathering information can go on indefinitely if you let it and become an unending quest unto itself. The time comes when you realize that information is being duplicated or that you have covered enough bases to construct a wise plan and it's time to sit down to assess your options.

Which options align with your values? Which options seem best suited to your strengths? Which options are most viable with the resources available to you? Which options just plain make sense? Do the wisest sages in your life agree?

Phase 3: Select a Plan

I've watched people become afflicted with "paralysis by analysis" and I think I've had mild cases of it myself a time or two. Sometimes the paralysis exists for fear of selecting the wrong plan or fear of not being able to carry out the plan or fear that there is a better plan out there or the fear of how the plan will be received by others. So a plan never gets acted on—"paralysis by analysis."

Rarely is there such a thing as a perfect plan because plans are made by imperfect people. The time comes when you simply say, "Okay, I've done my homework and with the information available to me at this time, this plan makes the most sense." Besides, remember, it is a course-plotting loop; the plan will be reviewed and revised along the way.

Phase 4: Create Action Steps, Set Timelines, Establish Real Accountability
  and Consequences

What steps do you need to take for the plan to be realized and in what order should they be taken? Sit down, put it on paper, and then write the steps on your calendar. When will the steps be taken? Knowing what you will do is great, knowing when you will do it, is equally important. If you leave the steps to chance, chances are you won't take them. If you think you need to wait for the perfect setting, under a perfect sky, on a perfect day, you will wait until you die.

Put date night with your spouse on the calendar in ink. Schedule the jog or workout and make it next to non-negotiable. Make the appointment with the financial planner. Just figure out what you need to do and when you will do it.

Then, if you are serious, really serious, if you truly want to do more than simply say you have a plan, show your plan to a friend, business partner, or mentor. Ask them to review it, comment on it, and then hold you accountable to do it with some built-in consequences if you don't. Your plan already has built-in rewards of greater financial freedom, better relationships, stronger health…but what about the consequences for not following the plan? Put some teeth in your plan.

I went through a season with my staff where we had a plan to meet every Tuesday morning at 11:30 for our weekly team meeting. Over time, people started getting lax about showing up on time, then more lax and more lax still. Showing up 5–15 minutes tardy or wandering in more than 20 minutes late offering lame excuses about phone calls, the line at the microwave, or the slow service at the drive-through window at Taco Bell. We had a plan to meet at a designated time, but the plan had no teeth. So, one day, when I sat alone at 11:30 waiting for my staff to drift in, I found myself getting more frustrated by the minute with the inconsideration of others, the lack of honoring commitments, and the disrespect of other people's time. Then suddenly I was inspired with a little incisor-canine-like idea. When the last offender straggled in, I announced that beginning next Tuesday we were going to be commitment keepers. We would be considerate of the schedules of others. We would show respect by being fully present and seated at the conference table by 11:30 am sharp. I announced there would be consequences for any and all tardiness or absences not personally signed off by me in advance… financial consequences. The consequence for being late from 11:30:01– 11:35 was a flat fee of $5 and every minute after that $1.00. The money would be put in a pot and given to the building fund. An amazing transformation overcame the staff and the very next Tuesday what they had once been so careless about they were suddenly very intentional about. The "unavoidable" scheduling conflicts and unexpected phone calls were now suddenly manageable. It is amazing what a powerful motivator consequences can be. The issue of chronic lateness just disappeared and now is a nonissue.

If you are really truly serious about getting the kind of results you want to see with your plan, give it some teeth. Fail to show up at the corner on time to meet your walking/jogging partner…you buy them dinner at Bonefish Grill. Neglect to schedule that appointment with the financial planner, you mow your accountability partner's yard. Don't complete an assignment on time, your partner takes possession of your iPod. Miss a date night with your spouse, they get a brand new 31 foot Beneteau or whatever floats your boat! You get the idea. Most everything in life will get done more timely with action steps, timelines, accountability, and consequences. Some things will only get done that way. Don't kid yourself on this one, get some accountability, establish consequences, or stay frustrated.

Execute

Now that you have a plan, do it. Just do it. Don't be like the man who had a target to shoot at, and kept saying, "Ready, aim…ready, aim…ready, aim…" and never got around to pulling the trigger because something always kept him from saying "fire."

Take the initiative. *You* call the financial planner, set the appointment, and get your retirement fund started. *You* make the child care arrangements, so the date night can happen. *You* make sure the right food is in the house and the wrong food out the door, so the diet can be adhered to. *You* take the responsibility to make sure the action steps get taken in a timely fashion. This means that *you* will be the initiative taker.

Question: Ultimately, whose responsibility is it to see that you have a nest egg waiting for you at retirement? Your company's? Your parents'? Your investment planner's? Or you? It's *you*!

Likewise, ultimately, whose responsibility is it to see that you have a fully connected marriage; that your body is in shape; that values are being instilled in your kids; or that your career is advancing? It's your responsibility, right? If not yours, then whose? Your spouse's? Your boss's? Your parents'? Your friends'? It's yours. You must take responsibility for your life. You can whine, you can blame fate, circumstances, or other people; but whining and blaming will never get you where you want to go or make you into who you want to be. Or you can take responsibility for yourself and take the initiative. If you wait for the perfect moment, in the perfect setting, under a perfect sun, you will wait until you die...Execute the plan.

Review and Revise

As we sailed to the restaurant and back to the marina, on that beautiful winter day, the wind was swallowed by a building high pressure system and just died. Flat out, dead calm. A beautiful day if you're water skiing or fishing on a power boat, but not so great if you are sailing. So before leaving the dock at the restaurant, we had to revise our plans and fire up the good old "iron ginny" and motor home. Fortunately, I had prepared for that contingency and had plenty of fuel on board.

Sailing is a sport that demands periodic course assessments and corrections. So does life. Sometimes the winds will shift on you and you'll need to adjust the sails a little. Other times, there will be a finger of the wind gusting a few hundred yards away, and a slight course correction will put extra power in your sails. And then there are times the wind totally shifts direction and you've got to re-plot your course. Then, of course, sometimes the wind gets swallowed up entirely and you lean into contingency plans. The point is with sailing and usually with life, you must review your plan, make course corrections to take advantage of an opportunity that presents itself, adjust to shifting winds in the market place, catch a financial investment gust, or address a stormy relationship. Wise and experienced sailors have, as a part of their plan, the periodic review and revision of their plan.

Fail to do this in your life, and even though you may have much to be grateful for…odds are your career will fail to reach full potential; your marriage will not be as connected at a soul-level with the consistency that you desire; or you may not uncover a health concern in a timely fashion.

So, periodically, maybe once a quarter (often enough to stay on top of things, but not so frequent you end up micro-managing), step out of things, gather some hard facts, and make some very honest assessments as to how things are going. How things are going…really. Are you on target with the career plan? What is the true state of your marriage? Is this the relational doldrums that every marriage seems to go through or is something else going on? Is this simply a market course correction or the beginning of a recession? What can be better leveraged? Where are there even stronger opportunities? Where are things losing momentum?

One of the first jobs of a leader is to state reality. So, as you lead your life, what you need are the cold, hard, accurate, and objective facts. Not what you wish was the case, but accurate information, so you can make honest evaluations and make any necessary course corrections to either better leverage opportunities and/or address challenges early on before they grow into a disaster looming on your bow. Be street smart. Stay dialed in. Be honest and proactive.

Rarely are things a straight sail to any destination. So where you need to, adjust the position of the relational sails, or raise more parenting sails to catch a favorable opportunity with a child. Be wise enough to tweak, adjust, or re-plot your direction and be courageous enough to change your course entirely, if necessary. Review, revise, and then continue around the loop again. Execute the revised plan and sail on. Next quarter, review and revise again, if needed…the learning loop.

Captain's Log

I know both the rewards and regrets when it comes to course plotting.

One of my bigger regrets is not putting these "plotting my course"

principles into practice at an early stage in the financial realm of my life.

Today, I follow a rock solid plan that works as long as I work the plan.

That plan is 10–10–80. The first 10% of all you earn goes to the work of

God at the church you attend. This brings God's blessings to bear on your

finances and who doesn't want that. Then, 10% gets invested for the future.

(One day you will want to scale back on work and maybe retire.) And,

then, you live on the remaining 80%.

Another principle I failed to practice until late in the game is to live

within your means or do not spend more than you earn—avoid debt like

the plague. Wise Solomon said, "…the borrower is servant to the lender."

And boy was he right! Finally, get on the right side of interest. Interest can

be a very intense friend or a very intense enemy. I knew a woman once who

had a very intense personality. If she was your friend, then she was really

your friend. Loyal, supportive, willing to do anything, anytime, anyplace

for you, if you were her friend. If you were her enemy, then you really were

her enemy. She was cold, calculated, and vindictive. Once, when I saw the

intensity with which she dealt with someone who crossed her, I thought

"Wow, I'm glad she's my friend, because I sure wouldn't want this woman

for an enemy." If interest were a person it would be this woman.

Get on the right side of interest and you can go on a financial joy ride.

Get on the wrong side and it can literally wreck your life.

Ruminate on this little $3,000 scenario and then choose wisely. If

you were carrying $3,000 in credit card debt and decide to pay it back in

minimum monthly payments (2% of the unpaid balance at 18% interest), do you realize how long it would take to pay it off and how much you would pay before you were through? Ready? What do you think, three years? Seven? 13? 20? Nope, nope, nope, and nope. It would take 30 years and 10 months and you would end up paying $10,396 by the time you are through. (Talk about paying stupid-tax!)

Now, flip that around and let's say you had $3,000 in hand that you invested in an IRA yielding 10% interest and you never added another dime to it. You just let it sit and accumulate interest over 30 years and 10 months. Any idea how much money you would have waiting for you at the end of that time period? Would you double it? Triple it? Quadruple it? Nope, nope, and nope. The answer is $65,743. Interest is interesting isn't it? Interest is an intense friend or an intense enemy.

Plot your course, plot it wisely. Make sure you are sailing to the right destination. This is your life, your one and only life.

- 5 -

Sage Advice from Some Old Salts

I find the great thing in this world is not so much where

we stand, as in what direction we are moving.

To reach the port of heaven, we must sail sometimes

with the wind and sometimes against it.

But we must sail, and not drift, nor lie at anchor.

—OLIVER WENDELL HOLMES

S pend some time around a marina or onboard a sailing vessel and pretty soon, you'll start to hear some of the old salts passing on wisdom of the sea via adages and proverbs. Sayings like:

+ "Red sky at night, sailor's delight. Red sky in morning, sailors take warning."

+ "Ring around the moon, rain is coming soon."

+ "Smooth seas do not make skillful sailors."

+ "The higher the clouds, the better the weather."

+ "Mackerel skies and mares' tails, soon it will be time to shorten sails."

All my adult life, I have intentionally sought out and made sure that I had relationships established with a few people who were older, more experienced, and further down the road of life than me. Some of these relationships have been personal and close. Others, unknown to them, served as mentors from a distance through their writings and teachings. From these sages, I have gleaned a world of insight, wisdom, and knowledge. They have challenged me to reach full potential as a husband, father, and leader. They have served as a personal board of directors in times of decision and direction seeking. They have helped shape my character and contributed to who I am and what I have accomplished with my life.

From countless hours of sitting in coffee shops talking, conversing over a phone, listening to conference speakers, or reading books, certain wise sayings have stuck with me. They have served me well, and I pass them on with the hope that they will do the same for you.

1. If you keep on doing more of what you are already doing, you'll just keep on getting more of what you've already got.

2. Measure twice, cut once.

3. Where there is no more wood the fire goes out. Know when to stop throwing logs on a heated quarrel.

4. Outside of God's grace, people tend to only become more and more of who they already are.

5. A person's recent past is the best predictor of their near future.

6. God parts the water, as you walk into it, not as you look at, not as you debate, not as you move toward it, but as you walk into it.

7. Only, only marry an emotionally healthy, growing Christian or you will live to regret it.

8. If it seems too good to be true, overwhelming odds are it is too good to be true.

9. If you wait till the perfect moment on the perfect day, with the perfect plan, you'll wait till you die.

10. Out pray the problem; out last the opposition.

11.   Get on the solution-side of things.

12.   Can a leopard change its spots?

13.   Be as wise as a serpent and as harmless as a dove.

14.   Bad company really does corrupt good character.

15.   How many holes does it take to sink a ship? (Just one) How big does that hole have to be? (Not very big, it's just a matter of time.) Big hole, you sink fast; little hole, you sink slow. But either way, you end up in the drink. Keep your life "hole free."

16.   You'll always miss 100% of the swings you don't take.

17.   God will always reward those who seek Him diligently.

18.   Only one life will soon be past, only what's done for Christ will last.

19.   I'd rather fail at something I truly believe in, than succeed at something I didn't.

20.   First rule of the Mounted Cavalry: If your horse is dead, dismount and ride another.

21.   Pray as if it all depended on God, work as if it all depended on you.

22.   Borrow the scar-tissue of others.

23.   Avoid paying stupid-tax.

24.   You are what you do, you do what you think. Think wisely.

25.   You have never locked eyes with someone who doesn't matter to God.

26.   Before you speak, ask yourself: Is it true? Is it kind? Is it necessary?

27.   Out of the abundance of the heart, the mouth speaks.

28.   What gets measured and rewarded, is what gets done.

29.   Don't treat symptoms, find a cure.

30. People both appreciate and resent strength and success in others; for the same reasons strong, successful people are both admired and attacked.

31. If you can't out persuade them, out last them.

32. The road you are on determines where you end up.

33. If you can't fix it, feature it.

34. The best fruit is out on the end of the limb.

35. God can be trusted, fully and completely, but not manipulated.

36. The higher the levels, the greater the devils.

37. Mistakes can be the portals of discovery.

38. This, too, will pass.

39. Treat people like they matter, and your life will matter.

40. Never let fear and self-doubt make you a prisoner.

41. Never say someone's "no" for them.

42. If you honor God, God will honor you.

43. Excellence honors God and attracts people.

44. The definition of insanity is to keep on doing the same thing, in the same way, over and over yet expect different results.

45. Live for today, but plan for tomorrow.

46. Knowing doesn't make the difference—doing does.

47. Show me your friends and I'll show you your future.

48. Under promise, over deliver.

49. Today's decisions create tomorrow's experiences.

50. Wise mentors work magic.

51. Be a lifelong learner.

52. Pay attention to what you pay attention to.

53. How you spend your time is how you spend your life.

54. Take care of your stuff.

55. Simplify.

56. Don't make mountains out of molehills.

57. Better to dig for facts than jump to conclusions.

58. Seek to understand, then to be understood.

59. Think "win-win."

60. Most times "good" really is the enemy of "great."

61. You eat an elephant one bite at a time...so start chewing.

62. Be the bigger person.

63. Be yourself...the best version of yourself.

64. Look people in the eye and offer a firm handshake.

65. The only place success comes before work is in the dictionary.

66. Wonderful opportunities often show up disguised as problems.

67. You either control your attitude or your attitude controls you.

68. Your attitude, your choice.

69. Always speak the truth...in loving ways.

70. Hurt people...hurt other people.

71. Finish the job.

72. Forgive, learn from, let go, and move on.

73. If you don't start, it's certain you won't arrive.

74. Look for opportunities, not guarantees.

75. You don't have to attend every argument you are invited to.

76. Don't swap your dreams for regrets.

77. The naked truth is always better than a well-dressed lie.

78. Wisdom is to receive the wisdom of the wise.

79. Facts and reality are your friends.

80. In much counsel there is wisdom.

81. Walk with the wise, grow wise; run with fools, suffer harm.

82. To get the right decisions, get the right people around the table.

83. It is not enough to do your best, you must know what to do, then do your best.

84. Have a bias toward action.

85. Fool me once, shame on you. Fool me twice, shame on me.

86. Be a thermostat, not a thermometer.

87. Sometimes it's just best to let sleeping dogs lay.

88. Keep your promises.

89. As a dog returns to its vomit, so a fool to his folly. (Proverbs 26:11)

90. Faithful are the wounds which come from true friends.

91. Your system is perfectly designed to get the results you are currently experiencing.

92. Admitting your mistakes makes you a better person and gains the respect of others.

93. As long as there is life and breath and God there is hope, and if God is really in it, the first two are optional.

94. You always, always reap what you sow.

95. Guard your heart, everything flows from it.

96. Go until you get a "no."

97. The decisions you make…make you.

98. Keep your "stop doing" list up to date.

99. It's okay to dream while you sleep, just don't sleep through your dreams.

100. Direction and action—not intentions—determine destination.

101. *It* doesn't work—you work *it*!

PART II

Ship Mates

- 6 -

Crossing Relational Seas

There are those who pass like ships in the night, who meet for a moment,
then sail out of sight with never a backward glance of regret;
folks we know briefly then quickly forget.
Then there are friends who sail together, through quiet waters
and stormy weather, helping each other through joy and through strife.
And they are the kind who give meaning to life.

—UNKNOWN

For months leading up to our 20th wedding anniversary, your mom and I daydreamed about our trip to beautiful St. Lucia, one of the Windward Islands in the southern Caribbean. We had booked a cottage overlooking Marigot Bay, planned a few sightseeing trips, and chartered a sailboat for a couple of days. All made even better with the prospect of taking this adventure with a couple of close friends who would accompany and celebrate with us; the kind of friends who somehow find ways to double your joys and half your sorrows.

The whole prospect seemed like one of those "pinch-me-can-this-really-be-true" deals. I must admit the piece I looked forward to the most was the chartered sails. Up to that point, my sailing had been limited to day sails around Tampa Bay and a few quick runs out into the Gulf of Mexico and back. Enjoyable, but overall safe, forgiving, and within the grasp of even novice sailors. I anticipated that the Caribbean Sea would offer a little sailing 301 and I was not disappointed.

The night before the sail, I was so amped I could hardly sleep. Of course, I was up early and eager to get out on the high seas. After we stocked up at the provisions store, we launched with our chartered captain and first mate—a couple of St. Lucians who had done this drill countless times with tourists just like us, from all over the world.

The sail north was all the adrenaline rush I had hoped. We were reaching against a 15–18 knot wind and eight foot rolling seas with me at the helm. Wow! What a blast! We sailed into Rodney Bay, ventured ashore, had lunch, toured the British Fort, shopped, and returned to the boat. As we crawled into the cockpit, our captain and first mate were sound asleep down below in the cabin. Only after we made a racket and talked loudly did they stir and stumble up the passage way ladder. Their eyes, speech, and demeanor were a dead give away that while we were ashore, they were getting wasted. My first thought was, "Oh boy, this will give new definition to sailing the high seas." Second thought, "Can this intermediate sailor from Safety Harbor, get this 45 foot boat home to Marigot Bay, if necessary?" Third thought, "If we make it back safely, I will never, never ever sail with these ya-hoos again." Long story short, we made it back. Interesting trip, but we made it. Believe me, I was remarkably grateful we only had a two or three hour run with the wind somewhere between aft and breach. I couldn't imagine being stuck with the St. Lucian version of Cheech and Chong for a few days in the small confines of a sailboat. Not much room to avoid or create physical distance on a vessel at sea.

What a great lesson—choose your land crew with the same kind of intelligence and intuition which you would use to choose your sailing crew. Decide who you will do life with using the same level of wisdom and discernment as those you would sail with. The wrong crew can turn even the most ideal sailing conditions into an endurance contest that you think will never end and conversely the right crew can make for a great time even when the conditions are far from perfect.

The same is so very true in any endeavor in life. The right business partners or coworkers can make even the most challenging times in your career manageable. The wrong people can make you dread Mondays even when things are going up and to the right. The right relationships can double your joys and half your sorrows. The wrong relationships can make it seem like the opposite happens—your joys are halved and your sorrows doubled.

So let's talk relationships in general, then dial in on a couple of key relationships you will have in your life. The wise sage, Solomon, offers some tried and tested wisdom on relationships. He urges us to be very cautious and wise in the establishment of relationships. "The righteous choose their friends carefully..." he says in Proverbs 12:26. For better or for worse, those you let into your life, those you get closest to and spend time with, will exert some of the greatest influence on your life. Values, attitudes, outlook on life, language, and behavior all get shaped and impacted by those closest to you. The more time you spend around these people, the greater the likelihood that who they are will begin to rub off on you. So, be very cautious and very wise about who your ship mates are. And be very diligent about the friendships your children make...bad company really can and does corrupt good character. If you see your kids hooking up with the wrong kind of influences, notice attitudes beginning to turn south...love them enough to step in and make some tough decisions for them before they get too far down a wrong path.

Solomon mentions six qualities to look for in ship mates, be they a spouse, a friend, a business partner, or associate. His wisdom will serve you well.

Loyalty

"A friend loves at all times…" Proverbs 17:17

We all seem to have the understanding that spouses, friends, and partners should be loyal to one another. They honor each other, whether or not the other is present. They rise up to protect the name and reputation of the other. They are loyal to their word. Loyal to commitments. Loyal to values and would never ask you to compromise on your integrity or standards.

There are few relational hurts that go deeper than betrayal by one you trust. So, as you are building a relationship, if you see the person display a lack of loyalty in speech or action to other friends, an employer, or a spouse…consider it a huge warning flag and be cautious. I had a friend once who I knew had been disloyal to two spouses and at least one employer, but I naively thought he would never do the same to me. Besides, I got so much value from our discussions over coffee. Boy was I ever wrong, for the day came when I paid so much "stupid-tax" for overlooking his character flaw.

Persevering Spirit: Stick-to-it-tiveness

"Do not forsake your friend or a friend of your family…" Proverbs 27:10

Life can be hard. Business can go through heart-stopping down turns. Health can deteriorate. Marriage has its dry seasons and you may find yourself wondering, "Why did I commit all my love for the rest of my life to this person?!"

When life gets hard, really hard and maybe for what seems like a really long time, this is when you really find out who is a real friend and who is not. Acquaintances will watch from a distance, associates will check out, and fair weather friends will fade away. But, those with a persevering spirit will stay true blue. They won't leave you in a lurch nor abandon you. They just flat out refuse to give up on you or the relationship.

The only kind of person you want to go through the ups and downs of life with is someone with a persevering spirit. If early on in a relationship, you notice you are getting hooked up with someone who gives up when things get a little hard or quits when the challenges are a little too great, be very cautious and wise about how close you get to them. Storms will roll into your life, things will get hard and odds are someone with a history of quitting will quit on you, too. And odds are a person with a proven track record of persevering will look you in the eye and say we're riding this storm out together. No jumping ship for me. If we go down, we go down together.

An Even-tempered Nature

"Do not make friends with the hot-tempered..." Proverbs 22:24

You let a hot-tempered person onboard and you can just about count on conflict, strife, arguments, and blowups and all on a fairly regular basis. Oh, and don't kid yourself here, either. Don't think that you will be the exception. Don't think that the hot-tempered person will only direct their steam at others and not you. That's not very realistic thinking, it's only a matter of time and circumstances. You will end up going toe-to-toe over something or you'll find yourself walking on eggshells for fear of setting off a land mine. Either way, it's a really lousy way to live.

Look for people who show signs of emotional health. Even-tempered people don't over- nor under-react. People who are emotionally healthy give, as well as receive; they ride out highs and lows without going to extremes; they are healthy enough to recognize their emotional state, mature enough to manage their feelings, and take the necessary steps to process the things that ding and wound their spirit.

You can spare yourself a lot of grief, headaches, and even heartaches by making sure those who are closest to you are even-tempered.

A Truth-speaker in Love

"Wounds from a friend can be trusted…" Proverbs 27:6

One of the first jobs of a leader is to "state reality." Leaders don't understate nor overstate things. They call things as they really are, not as they wish they were. They say it in a manner that convinces those they lead that they truly have their best interest at heart. Leaders say it in a way that inspires hope not despair. They say it in a way that builds up and avoids tearing down. They speak the truth in love.

You and your best ship mates in life will do this for each other. The truth gets spoken in loving ways. If you get things out of balance on the "in love" side, all you will have is a pleasant little, mutual admiration society. Truth be told, you'll probably never reach full potential as a person unless you have people in your life who will love you enough to tell you when you are drifting in your values or compromising on your morals. You need someone who will call you on the carpet when you shade the truth or mishandle others. You want someone who will point out the blind spots in your parenting or marriage. You'll find most people hesitate to do this for fear it will jeopardize or compromise the whole relationship, but where relationships are real you can be real with each other.

Wisdom

> *"...the pleasantness of a friend springs from their heartfelt advice."*
> Proverbs 27:9

> *"Walk with the wise and become wise, for a companion of fools*
> *suffers harm." Proverbs 13:20*

It is no secret that life has its share of complications and complexities. At times, the options and variables can feel like a virtual maze and at those times, you will most likely lean into those around you for counsel and advice as you sort these things out. You will hope they know both you and life well enough to provide insight that is valuable and counsel that is timely. When you are making decisions about raising your kids, the handling of finances, negotiating a relationship, or a business deal, you want people in your life whose advice is full of wisdom. You want people who have a solid history of making wise decisions.

Sharp

> *"As iron sharpens iron, so one person sharpens another."*
> Proverbs 27:17

I once heard someone ask these questions: "Which would you rather shave with? A dull razor or a sharp razor? Which would you rather cut down a tree with? A dull saw or a sharp saw? And which TV would you rather watch? One with dull color and clarity or one with a sharp picture?" The answer, of course, is "sharp" every single time, right?

So, my question is what kind of life do you want to lead? Dull or sharp? The right people in your life should make you sharper. They should challenge you to grow, and inspire you to reach full potential. They should help you develop and make you a better person. They should sharpen your intellect, skills, character, self-esteem, and your relationship with God. Ask yourself, "Will this person dull me down or sharpen me up?"

Before getting on board with business partners, friends, and certainly before committing the rest of your life to someone, run them by this little checklist.

+ Are they loyal, truly loyal?

+ Are they a persevering soul or a quitter?

+ Are they an even-tempered person?

+ Do they speak the truth in loving ways?

+ How wise are they really?

+ Will they help you reach your full potential in life?

Remember the words of Solomon. Be very wise and very cautious about who your ship mates are in life.

For the most part, people are who they are by their mid-twenties. Their character is pretty well set and usually they will become more and more of who they already are as they age. Yes, God can and does transform those who are willing, cooperate with Him, and establish support outside themselves, but rarely do people change much on their own. People can adjust their attitude and behavior for awhile, but once the pressure is off, they tend to revert to who they really are.

How do you find the right people to crew with in your life? To begin, you be that right crew member, first. Follow the Golden Rule: do unto others as you would have them do unto you. Take the initiative in going where the kind of people you want to meet can be found. Then take the initiative to introduce yourself to them. Over time, you will be amazed at the relationships with which you will be rewarded.

- 7 -

First Mate, Soul Mate

"If you want a good first mate, marry one."

—UNKNOWN

The decision on whom to marry is huge! The decision on whom you will enter into a lifelong commitment of love with is huge! Did I say *huge*?! Get it right and the odds of having a rewarding and fulfilling marriage will significantly increase. Get it wrong and the odds of heartbreak and frustration will simply skyrocket.

It is not too much to say that the single most important decision you will make in this life, outside of the decision to follow God, is the decision on whom to marry. It is a life-altering decision. It is a decision that can make or break quality-of-life issues. It is a decision that will impact most every area of your life.

I can think of friends who were bright and talented, and who achieved enviable levels of success in their chosen field of endeavor in the marketplace. They enjoyed all the benefits that success can bring—living in exclusive subdivisions, driving upper-end foreign cars, taking exotic trips, and such—but for any number of reasons their marriage was a mess.

So from the curb, their beautiful house said they had it made. But few knew that inside that house was a home of heartache and relational pain.

I think of one friend, in particular, whose marriage introduced so much pain and heartache in his life, that at one point he confided in me that he would trade all his success in the marketplace and all his possessions if it would mean true harmony in his marriage. My friend was simply echoing the wisdom of Solomon, who said, "Better a dry crust with peace and quiet than a house full of feasting, with strife." (Proverbs 17:1)

Fortunately, it doesn't have to be that way. Such was never God's intention for couples. God designed marriage in such a way that couples would grow into being soul mates. It is to be a place where you can know and be known at the deepest levels possible between two human beings. A place where you can love and be loved in the safe confines of unconditional commitment. A place of mutual serving and celebrating, a place where, as Scripture says, the two become one. And this is something way more than the beauty of physical oneness, it is oneness of heart and soul. A lover, a confidante, an encourager, a partner in life, and a mate of the soul.

It should be no surprise to anyone that marriages like that don't just happen. Strong marriages, like strong sports teams, strong businesses, and strong churches are the result of selecting the right people and working the right plan. That being so, the questions that beg to be asked, then answered are: "How does one go about selecting the right person?" and "What is the right plan to work?"

Let's start with the issue of selecting the right person. Wouldn't you agree that knowing what to look for in a spouse is a fairly important starting point? Sure it is! If you don't know what you are looking for, how in the world will you know when you find someone who could become your lifelong soul mate? Three words that will serve you well in your search are: character, compatibility, and chemistry.

Character

First, you have to know, is this a person of character? True character? Steady, dependable, trustworthy character. Would they graduate summa cum laude from character school? Do they unquestionably exhibit the six qualities from the shipmate checklist? Are they loyal, maybe even loyal to a fault with you? Do they have a persevering, never-give-up, I'll-do-whatever-it-takes-to-keep-love-alive spirit in them? What's their anger management like? How do they resolve relational conflicts? Do they always have to be right? Do they speak the truth to you, even hard truths; but in honoring, respectful, and loving ways? Where do they fall on the wisdom/common sense meter? Do they believe in you, really believe in you? And does being around them make you a better person?

If you can't give the person the highest marks in these areas, why would you want to enter into a binding, lifelong relationship with them? Oh, and don't you dare fall for the "once we get married she'll change... once we get married, he'll come around" myth. Overwhelming odds are...not going to happen! Instead, let me say it again: people who really want to be transformed can be by God's grace and power, but for the most part people usually become more and more of who and what they already are. So, ask yourself the hard questions like are there qualities about the person's personality or behavior that bother you? Things like jealousy, anger, irresponsibility, depression, lack of motivation, dishonesty, stubbornness, moodiness, or selfish narcissism? Then ask yourself, "Can I live with these characteristics for the rest of my life, if they never change?" If the answer is no, then why would you marry them?

Additionally, if there are any unresolved problems in their life with things like drugs, alcohol, or substance abuse, sexual infidelity, physical or sexual abuse...then my best advice is *run*, don't walk, *run* to the nearest exit. Marriage is a wonderful institution, but it is not a rescue mission nor a rehabilitation center. Marriage does not make difficulties and problems go away, instead it will most likely introduce a few new challenges and intensify the others that already exist.

Getting to know someone's true character takes time. It means seeing the person in times of low-stress and high-stress situations, in atmospheres of recreation and business, interactions with family, friends, and associates, in heavy traffic and joy rides. It takes time and a variety of circumstances to determine someone's character.

Compatibility

I've heard it said that every similarity that couples share is like money in the bank. Common interests in life make doing life together a little easier and certainly more enjoyable. Commonly held values really do give a more solid foundation upon which to make mutually agreed upon decisions. Common levels of energy, common ambition, and common recreational pursuits all add to making a marriage thrive. But the single greatest and most important ingredient where there needs to be similarity is spiritually. Scripture says that we should never compromise on this and become "unequally yoked" with someone. (A yoke is an apparatus that fits over the necks of oxen or some other beast of burden to keep them going in the same direction.) If you have chosen to follow God, then don't even think of "yoking up" with someone who is going to pull you away from Him. Make sure, really sure, whomever you marry does more than say they believe in

God. Make sure they show signs of being fully devoted to Him. Make sure they walk the talk. Don't compromise on this one; you will pay for it if you do. My mantra: only marry an emotionally healthy, growing Christian. Period!

Compatibility does not mean marrying a clone of yourself, (how boring would that be?). Rather marry someone who is enough like you to be compatible, but also different enough to be complimentary to you. We all have our strengths and weaknesses, we all have our preferential likes and dislikes...and managed correctly this is what can add spice to life and strength to marriage.

I'm a mild extrovert who gets energy from people and activity; your mom is a mild introvert who seeks a little solitude and silence when she needs renewal. I make decisions with my head and want facts and explanations. For a decision to be right for your mother, it must "feel right" because she processes things through her heart. I'm a structured person who wants a sense of order, neatness, strategic planning, and single focus. Your mom is unstructured and can thrive in what feels like clutter to me; she can be quite comfortable multi-tasking and freelancing. I learn best visually, your mom by doing the activity hands on. Maybe opposites really do attract.

So, even though we share the common foundational stones of marriage, we are anything but clones of each other. When we acknowledge, honor, and respect these personality differences it makes us so much stronger together than we are separately because we compliment each other. Managed wrongly they are a source of frustration, agitation, and conflict. What makes us compatible is that we share a common foundation. What makes us stronger is we choose to embrace the uniqueness of each other's personalities as a compliment to our own.

Chemistry

This is the relational spark, the physical attraction, the "you-made-me-look-twice" dynamic. When God made us and hard wired into us what it means to be human, He saw fit to create an attraction to the opposite sex. With some people, we will have an appreciation for who they are, but have about as much of a spark as a book of water-soaked matches. Some will create a spark or a short-lived flame of interest, but a select few will have 4th of July fireworks potential.

So, long ago and far away, I was a college student standing in the hallway talking with friends between classes. Who should walk by but one shapely brunette with man-killer blue eyes and a certain confident, sassy strut to her walk. (Sparks!) I had to find out who she was, so I inquired around and negotiated a face-to-face introduction. (Flames!) After a few dates, I moved in for a good-night kiss. (Fireworks!) And after more than a quarter of a century of marriage, your mom can still catch my eye, raise my heart rate, and ignite the 4th of July.

Never marry on the basis of chemistry alone (chemistry does not conquer all), but also never marry unless there is some chemistry present. Married life is not five-alarm, blow-torch passion every night, but neither should you expect nor accept a passionless marriage.

Selecting the right person is not a guarantee in itself that you will have a lifelong soul mate, but it certainly and significantly increases the odds of such. You'll raise the odds even more by having a wise plan for marital connectedness that you work religiously.

Your mom and I had the importance of this branded into our souls early on in our marriage when we watched close friends of ours shipwreck their marriage. When we got word that their marriage was on the rocks, we were totally shocked as we naively thought they had an ideal marriage. Appearances really can be deceiving can't they?

We tried our best to help salvage their marriage, but by the time we got involved it had been so damaged by a duplicitous life and an extra-marital affair that they became yet another couple who joined Davy Jones' locker at the bottom of the deep blue sea.

When we sat down separately with our friends, we heard a story of a husband and wife who once led intertwined lives that over time became parallel lives, then separate lives, until finally they were two ships who passed in the night. Their jobs kept them apart all day, and they both were pursuing advanced educational degrees that kept them apart most week nights and every Saturday. If that wasn't enough, he coached on the side and she immersed herself in volunteer work. They sat side by side on Sundays in church, but that was about the only time. No time for conversations of the heart. No room for the kind of quantity of time it takes to enjoy quality time together. Then one day it happened; she crossed paths with an old flame. She allowed him back into her mind, then into her heart, and finally her life.

As your mom and I listened to the story of their journey, we were very shocked to realize we were in the early stages of following that same course. Our jobs, like most, kept us apart weekdays. She was pursuing a master's degree, while I worked on ordination into ministry, which meant evenings and weekends were spoken for and we couldn't even sit in church together, because I was the pastor leading the service.

It rang our bell to realize we were on the same path our friends had just traveled, only just not as far along. So we asked ourselves, "Why would this path lead us to a different destination than our friends?"

(Remember: Direction *not* intention determines destination.) "Why would we be an exception?"

So, we sat down and did some course correcting. We reaffirmed that we want to sail through life together and not just as roommates who live under the same roof, but as soul mates who are "one." Out of that time came a plan that we have been working for decades now. It has served us well, and perhaps our plan or one similar will serve you well, too. Our plan can be summed up in four words: sow, serve, solve, and secure.

Sow...good relational seeds

First, if you want your spouse to be your soul mate, you must always be about the business of sowing good relational seeds. The old adage really is true: you reap what you sow. This is true in every realm of life—career, health, finances, education, and marriage.

I spent incalculable hours not only on my grandparents' farm, but also farming for an agricultural company every summer during my college years. One unalterable principle I observed is that we always and only reaped what we sowed in the ground. Where my grandparents planted potatoes in the ground, they always only reaped potatoes. Never carrots, nor asparagus. And when they put corn seed in the ground each spring, come fall they harvested, guess what...that's right, corn. You reap what you sow. You can't sow wheat seed and expect to reap sorghum. Planting milo in the ground will never result in a harvest of watermelons.

As obvious as all this is, it never ceases to amaze me how smart, well-educated people think they can violate this principle of sowing and reaping in their relationships and not suffer any ill effect because of it. It's just nuts to behave this way, but nevertheless, husbands will speak in demeaning ways, fail to pull their weight with household chores, be non-responsive to requests, be non-communicative except to issue complaints, and then with that low level of emotional and communicational intimacy wonder why there is a low level of intimacy in the bedroom and a high level of dissatisfaction in the marriage. You reap what you sow. Plain and simple. In the same way, wives nag, complain, let themselves go, use disrespectful looks and tones, issue snide remarks, then wonder why their husbands are not more involved with them and the family? Why isn't he taking the lead? Why is he so distant?

If you want a spouse who is a soul mate and not a room mate, then you'll have to sow the kind of seeds that produce that kind of relationship. Seeds such as:

- Patience with the other's shortcomings

- Finding the kind way to say even the hardest truths

- Honoring each other's opinions and preferences

- Being very slow to become angry

- No record keeping of wrongs

- Celebrating each other's successes and accomplishments

- Protecting each other's honor, dignity, and reputation

- Demonstrating trust

- Always thinking the best of the other (this is *huge!*)

- Demonstrating a persevering, I'll-never-give-up-on-you-or-this-relationship spirit

- Saying the words "I love you" daily

- Having respectful voice tones, words, and looks

- Having a weekly date night, that is a lock on your calendar (no kids allowed)

- Attending marriage enrichment seminars or encounters
- Taking an over night trip somewhere once a quarter (no kids allowed here, either)
- Taking walks together
- Finding a recreational pursuit you both enjoy
- Communicating by phone, text, or email everyday

Every good seed you sow in your marriage is like money in the bank.

Serve...each other's needs

We all have needs; be they emotional, physical, intellectual, spiritual, or sexual. Most of us enter into marriage with the underlying expectation that marriage partners will be aware of and responsive to each other's needs. They will serve each other by seeking to meet their spouse's needs. When this happens, couples grow to deeper and deeper levels as soul mates. But when couples fail to serve each other by not meeting their partner's needs it can lead to frustration, disappointment, conflict, withdrawal, and worse...one or both partners looking outside the bonds of marriage for need fulfillment.

Soul mates seek to know, understand, and meet needs in ways that are meaningful to their spouse. It probably comes as no surprise that a husband's needs and a wife's needs vary from one another. Sometimes they may even vary greatly. If you truly want a soul mate for a spouse, it means engaging in open conversations to discover each other's needs, to find out how to best meet those needs, and then doing your best to serve your spouse accordingly.

Some of the most common and important needs couples long to have fulfilled by their partners are:

+ Communication
+ Companionship
+ Respect
+ Support
+ Affection
+ Sexual fulfillment

Communication

All of us long to know and be known, to understand and be understood. And no one is more important to experience this with than your spouse. This happens only through open, honest conversations where you really listen and really open up to talk. Some refer to communication as the secret to staying in love. (More on this later in this chapter.)

Companionship

No one enters into the lifelong commitment of marriage with the anticipation of flying solo through career obligations, educational pursuits, spiritual development, extended family gatherings, recreational pursuits, exercise programs, or parent-teacher conferences. We want a companion to experience the ins and outs and ups and downs of life together with us. This calls for some give and take and a willingness to step outside of our comfort zone. It may mean stretching yourself and watching a football game or going to a romantic movie. It could mean learning an appreciation for fishing or off-Broadway plays.

Soul mates find a way to "get into" what their spouse is "into" simply because they are "into their spouse."

Respect

Respect communicates value. Respect communicates honor. And who doesn't want to feel valued and honored, especially by your spouse. Every respectful look, every respectful tone or word, and every respectful action you offer your spouse is a positive deposit made in the marriage relational bank. It means respecting each other enough to listen, to put down the paper or push aside multi-tasking, and truly listen when the other is speaking. It means respecting the preferences of the other and not badgering nor attempting to wear the other down. It means respecting each other's opinions, ideas, and contributions. It means finding a way to disagree in a respectful fashion, as well. You can just about determine the connectedness of a couple by measuring the level of respect they show each other. Not much is worse than spending a night out with a couple who display a despicable lack of respect for each other.

I remember being out with a couple once, where the husband seemed to have made an art form out of disrespecting his wife. She was the butt of his jokes, the object of his cutting remarks, and the star of his "can-you-believe-how-dumb-this-was" stories. The look in her eyes said her spirit was dying a little more with each of his disrespectful words. Needless to say, it was the one and only evening we spent with them. My biggest regret of the evening was that I didn't tell the big buffoon to knock it off. Unfortunately, your mom and I have also seen wives engage in the same sick behavior as this husband. Disrespect makes huge negative withdrawals from the relational bank and it doesn't take long for a marriage to become bankrupt in this kind of atmosphere.

Support

How important is structural support to a bridge. Very important, right? How critical are stays and stanchions to the mast of a sailboat? Really critical, right? Take away bridge pilings or mast stays and the first heavy load on the bridge or the first strong gust of wind...prepare for collapse.

If you can understand this, then you can understand how important it is that spouses support each other. Life can just get heavy at times, can't it? There are financial obligations, career demands, educational pursuits, domestic chores, child-rearing responsibilities, dream chasing, health concerns, church commitments, and the list could go on and on. Sometimes the load feels so heavy you think if one more task gets piled on my plate, if I hear one more discouraging report, if one more person needs something from me...I think my knees will buckle under the weight of all this and I will collapse.

In times like this, more than ever, we need some support. Someone to come along side us and put a shoulder under the burden we are carrying. Someone to roll up their sleeves and lend a hand. Someone to buttress us up with words of encouragement. Someone to undergird us with support, be it emotional, physical, financial, domestic, spiritual, or any other form. Who else is better suited to provide this kind of support than your spouse?

Truth be told, we all need support of one kind or another most all the time. And not just when the load seems too heavy, because even when things are going well the right support can make "good" become "great!"

That's why the wise sage, Solomon said, "Two are better than one, because they have a good return for their labor: if they fall down, they can help each other up. But pity those who fall and have no one to help them up! Also, if two lie down together, they will keep warm. But how can one keep warm alone? Though one may be overpowered, two can defend themselves. A cord of three strands is not quickly broken." Ecclesiastes 4:9-12.

So in positive, constructive, respectful, and solution-oriented ways, communicate where you could use some support from your spouse and knock yourself out to support them first.

Affection

Every affectionate look, word, or touch affirms your mate's self-esteem, communicates value, and says, "I enjoy you and doing life with you." Affection and sexual intimacy are often viewed as being the same thing. Not so! It's possible to be affectionate without being sexually intimate and likewise, it is possible to experience sexual relations with little to no affection. Affection may lead to sexual intimacy, but not necessarily so. Affection is a back rub that leads to nothing more than a back rub. A touch on the arm, a kiss on the back of the neck, or a hand held as an end unto itself and not as an avenue to the bedroom. Affection is the non-sexual communication that says, "I love and value you, for more than your body."

Sexual Fulfillment

When God created we human beings, He took great pleasure in creating us male and female. Hard-wiring us to be sexual beings. And when the experience of sexual oneness is the culmination of emotional, spiritual, and life oneness, it can be a profound experience that touches our soul with love, acceptance, and value in a way deeper than perhaps anything else; save for the love of God.

The sexual dimension of our life was designed to regularly and joyfully bring this kind of fulfillment to our lives. Unfortunately, as with most powerful things, the potential to have a reverse and negative effect is also a very real possibility.

For many couples, the sexual dimension of their marriage brings some of the greatest levels of frustration they feel in their life. If those times are not managed properly, it can lead to tension, arguments, and distance in the marriage and vulnerability to the temptation of unhealthy forms of acting out which only erode future intimacy inside marriage.

Paying attention to this dimension of your marriage must always stay on your radar screen. This means you'll have to be willing to once again have open, honest, and respectful conversations about the frequency, atmosphere, and expressions that best work for you. It means negotiating through the busy seasons of life. It means paying attention to meeting the other needs in your spouse's life, as well. You simply can't isolate and separate the sexual dimension from the rest of your marriage and expect fulfillment. In fact, usually the better the companionship, the better the communication, the better the respect, the support, and the better the affection (you know where I'm going here, don't you?), the better the sexual fulfillment.

So, what I've just talked about are six of the basic needs we humans live with. Six needs that when met, help secure and strengthen the bond of marriage. Six needs that when neglected, ignored, or intentionally denied only seem to communicate rejection, devaluing, and disrespect to the one you have committed the rest of your life to.

Now here's a very unfortunate and ironic thing I have observed over the years in couple after couple...after couple: During the courtship phase of a relationship, both parties seem very intent on meeting the needs of the other person. The communication is frequent and late into the night over the phone. Talk is about everything and anything. They are each other's favorite companion, in fact they sometimes invent reasons to do things together. Never has anyone shown such respect and support. Affectionate looks, words, and touches are as common as the sand on the beach. And the anticipation is that once they walk the aisle and get married, every night will be 4th of July fireworks in the bedroom.

Then comes the honeymoon phase where all these expectations get reinforced and you both are convinced that you will be the fairy tale couple who lives happily ever after.

Next, is the learning to live together in the daily grind of life phase. Oh man, do the dynamics begin to change as reality settles in. Some of her once cute quirks become an irritating weirdness. A few of his idiosyncrasies become annoying obsessions. Toss in kids, career, house payments, and over time the demands of life increase, energy wanes, frustration builds, and one or both are not as attentive to meeting the needs of the other as they once were. And sometimes, rather than having an open, honest, rational, and respectful conversation about how a wife could use a little more domestic support or how the husband is feeling a little frustrated sexually, hints get dropped. Sarcastic remarks are said. Statements with double meanings are made. Some of which get missed entirely, others ding, and a few infuriate. Still others try the silent treatment and when asked what's wrong say, "Oh, nothing." But inside are thinking, "What do you mean what's wrong...you know exactly what's wrong. My needs are not being met."

When this doesn't work, the decision is made to up the intensity of the message. And in a crazy line of reasoning, a person thinks either consciously or otherwise, "I'll show them." And they decide to use a negative hammer to pound away hoping it will bring positive results. This usually leads to accusations about not caring, verbal sparring matches, harsh and cutting words, slammed doors, and mistreatment. This may work for a moment, but not over time. Usually, instead of inspiring a spouse to be more attentive to their mate's needs, it de-motivates and the spouse finds it hard to *want* to meet the needs of one who browbeats and mistreats them. Isn't it crazy to think if I make your life more miserable, you will be inspired to make my life better? If I mistreat you, you'll want to treat me better? If I devalue you, you will value me more? If I fail to meet your needs, you will want to meet mine? Forgetting that "we reap what we sow," those kinds of seeds always reap more misery, more mistreatment, more devaluing, and more frustration.

Then, in an even crazier line of reasoning, we think "Well, obviously, I didn't send a strong enough message." And so we up the level of mistreatment, raising voice levels, and increasing the degree of dissonance. Only to further alienate and de-motivate your spouse to want to meet your needs. Some couples continue on in this vicious cycle until things escalate and they become more like bitter roommates looking for an out than they do a married couple looking to stay together and be soul mates. Unless somebody or something breaks the downward cycle, it's only a matter of time until molehills become mountains, optimism becomes despair, and "I can't imagine life without you" becomes "I can't imagine living the rest of my life like this."

How much better to simply, early on, engage in open, honest, and respectful communication. How much wiser to simply subscribe to the words of Jesus, who taught, "It is in giving that you receive." It is in the intentional understanding and meeting of your spouse's needs in ways that are meaningful to them that makes them feel truly loved and thereby inspired to meet your needs in a similar fashion. Depending on the current state of matrimony in your home, and depending on the levels of hurt and frustrations, a positive response may not be immediate. These things usually happen not over night, but over time. Be patient, persevere, and pray like crazy. Love can and does re-grow and deepen. This brings me to the next word in our plan.

Solve…your relational issues

Every marriage will go through the doldrums and face dry seasons. Every marriage will have its share of challenges, disagreements, and issues. There is no such thing as a perfect marriage. You simply can't put one imperfect person into a binding, lifelong commitment with another imperfect person and expect a perfect marriage. That relational math simply doesn't work no matter how you add it up.

So, true soul mates expect they will face "stuff" and have a plan in place to solve issues as they rise up. Some guidelines that have served your mom and me well are:

1.   Address things sooner, rather than later. In most cases, it is easier to deal with a molehill than it is a mountain. The longer you wait, the longer your thoughts turn and heat up on the mental rotisserie grill. The longer you wait, the more frustration builds. So, if you truly can't address things right then and there, mutually agree on a time and place to resolve things.

2.   Think the best. We can choose to put things in the best light or the worst light. The light we choose to see things in will shape both our emotions and our response. Always choose to think the best of your spouse, give them the benefit of the doubt, unless they have proven to be untrustworthy.

3.   Have an agreed upon set of values and parameters for the conversation. In other words, have a conversation about how you will have conflict conversations. Parameters to consider are: no personal attacks allowed, stay respectful, listen to one another, be solution oriented, disagree in agreeable kinds of ways, and one your mom and I had from day one, no matter how angry or frustrated we are, we never use the "D" word (divorce).

4.   Use conciliatory language. As you express yourself, avoid blaming and making accusatory statements like, "You are such a...jerk, slob, idiot, moron, etc." Instead, say things like, "When this happened, I felt... taken for granted, disrespected, vulnerable, dishonored, insecure, hurt, embarrassed, etc." Also, avoid using phrases such as, "you always..." and "you never...." It may seem that way at times, but no one always gets it wrong and never gets it right. Those kinds of blanket statements leave no room for negotiation nor benefit for the other's character.

5.   Each of you state the problem clearly to the other from your perspective. It may surprise you to discover it is possible to be arguing about two different things. As the other person speaks, your job is to simply listen. Really listen. As your spouse speaks, avoid thinking of your response or retort to them. Once they finish, ask questions to clarify and then say, "This is what I heard you say..." And mirror back their words to

them. If your spouse says, "Not quite," then ask for clarification and mirror back their words until they say, "Yes, that's it." It is so important that you not only understand *what* they are saying the issue is, but that they understand that *you* understand.

6.   Once you both understand the issue from each other's perspective, brainstorm possible solutions. And by the way, refrain from eye rolls, sighs, or comments like, "That will never work." Just get on the solution side of things.

7.   Next, with a spirit of consensus, whittle down the possible solutions until you come to an agreement on which one you will select to follow.

8.   Set a time frame in which you will both adhere to the solution and then reconvene at that point to discuss how the solution is working and whether or not any tweaking of that solution is in order. Or it could be that a new or different solution is needed.

9.   If you get stuck, don't stay stuck. It will only lead to increased dissonance in the marriage. Instead, go see an objective outside third party. Maybe, it's a respected mentor, a pastor, or a qualified Christian counselor. Someone wise enough to give discerning counsel and someone objective enough to see the big picture and speak truth to the two of you. Just don't stay stuck. Way too much is at stake for you, your spouse and, if you have children, your kids. These precious little ones are counting on you to figure it out and fix it. Once you have kids, it's no longer just about you and for better or worse the relationship you have with your child's mom or dad will profoundly affect, shape, and impact their lives. For the sake of everyone involved, there are times you have to work hard at your marriage, fight to save it, and persevere, trusting by faith that the breakthrough

will come. The only time divorce is an option to consider is when there has been infidelity, abuse, or the other person truly has deserted the relationship. If your spouse is not willing to seek outside counsel, then you go yourself and get some perspective and coping tools.

Now, if these conflict-resolution guidelines don't serve you well, then find some that do or create your own. I just know this plan works if you work the plan. Granted, it takes a level of maturity on the part of both of you to work this plan. The deal is you can solve your issues in this way or you can yell, scream, slam doors, accuse, glare, give the cold shoulder or the silent treatment, and only deepen your problems and escalate the issues at hand. It's up to you. What kind of relationship do you want? What do you want the atmosphere in your home to be like? You get to decide. Choose wisely how you solve your issues. But solve them.

Secure…your relational boundaries

Some people like to see how close they can get to the fire before they get burned; how far they can lean over the rail before they fall overboard. That might be fine and fun for some, but when it comes to your marriage, that's just plain dumb. Why in the world would you want to put yourself in a position where you would be vulnerable to something or someone that could erode or destroy your marriage? Why would you put yourself in a setting where you might find yourself tempted to cross a line that would violate your sacred vows to your spouse? Secure your boundaries. Early on in our marriage, Mom and I put some safeguards in place, not because we didn't trust each other but simply because we don't trust the power of an illicit desire or an impulse in a weak moment. We don't trust the way emotional and mental connectedness can begin, grow, and lead to an unhealthy sexual energy between a man and a woman. We don't trust the evil one who delights in destroying homes and marriages. We don't trust others who may be unaware of their own vulnerability or may have less than honorable intentions.

So, early on in our marriage, Mom and I put these boundaries in place:

+ We don't have a meal, a coffee, or ride alone in the car with someone of the opposite sex unless the other knows about it in advance and signs off on it. If the other has a check in their spirit or feels uneasy about it, then no bickering over it and no accusations about not trusting. We simply don't meet with the person.

+ No conversations of the heart with any other person of the opposite sex. Conversations of the heart lead to emotional connectedness, mental connectedness, and spiritual connectedness. Over time, that kind of connectedness can create a building desire to express itself in physical connectedness. A touch, a hug, a kiss on the cheek, and an underlying subtle sexual energy can build until, at the wrong moment in the wrong place, passion can overwhelm. Conversations of the heart are reserved for your spouse.

+ No secret admirers. Over the years we both have been the object of someone else's attention or affection. Someone who is overly friendly, flirtatious, tried to engage us as their confidante, always seemed to negotiate their way into our presence, was gift giving, or in one way or another expressed an unhealthy interest in us. Our deal is when we first dial into what is going on, we immediately dial the other in on that person who is being a little too friendly. Beyond that, if one of us has spotted something in someone else's behavior that makes us uncomfortable then regardless of how innocent one views it, the other respects the flag of warning and the boundary around that person gets widened and contact lessened. If one of us is being truly paranoid or jealous, that's a separate issue to be addressed. But respect the observations and requests of your spouse for an increased boundary around that person.

Mom and I have had our share of challenges that come with putting any two people with different temperaments together. We have had our share of bumps, our hard seasons of life, and a few trips through the marital doldrums. But we have done it together. We are soul mates because we continue to work hard to:

+ Sow good relational seeds
+ Serve each other's needs
+ Solve our relational issues
+ Secure our relational boundaries

- 8 -

Parenting the Crew

Every now and then, I've had my "responsibility bell" rung with the unexpected force of a swinging boom on an accidental jibe.

Late one summer afternoon, the Florida west coast sea breeze kicked up and I coerced your mom and the two youngest, Michael and Bethany, to go out for a quick sunset sail in spite of the fact that there was a possibility of some lingering storm cells in the area. We motored out of the marina and set sail to the north, while everyone sat on the rail portside enthralled with the beautiful array of colors as that big red ball sank into the horizon.

To my embarrassment, I too, was so caught up in God's sunray and cloud finger painting on the palate of the western horizon that I lost sight of the bigger picture…behind us to the southeast a storm cell was building and as I came about to head back to the marina, I realized, "Oh no, that storm is going to explode and converge at the marina at just about the same time we do." It was about then the first lightning bolt crashed and it sounded like someone had just shot a 357 magnum handgun next to my ear; a rather unsettling experience for me, and a bit terrifying for Mom. She gave me a look that, thankfully, I have only seen a few times in our married life. She quickly gathered her precious little ones, went down below to the cabin, and as she closed the hatch to leave me alone in the elements, she informed me that since I had gotten us into this mess, it was my responsibility to get us out of it.

Believe me, I felt the weight of the responsibility. After all, I was the one who insisted we go out for a sunset sail and I was the one who assured her that all the storms had either passed or died out for the day and I was the one at the helm who wasn't staying dialed into the surrounding circumstances. So now, I had three of the five most precious people on earth to me on a floating piece of fiberglass with a 30 foot lightning rod in the vicinity of an electrical storm.

As I scrambled about the deck reducing sail and securing loose lines, I was also shooting "flare prayers" heavenward and weighing out my options: (a) head back to the marina and sail into the teeth of the storm or (b) fire up the "iron ginny" and turn tail and run 90 degrees away from the storm cell. It felt like the decision was a no-brainer—I ran and prayed. Turned out to be the best decision I made that day. We stayed dry, out of harm's way, and once the storm cell passed, we sailed into our home port safe and sound.

There have been other times in my life where I have felt the weight of certain responsibilities I carry in life. In my late teens, I worked for a farm corporation and after proving myself for a season, I had more and more responsibility placed in my lap until I was leading a work crew with some very expensive equipment and a valuable crop entrusted to me. I remember one little pep talk a corporate guy gave me, which went something like, "We're trusting you with $100,000 worth of machinery and a crop worth even more. We're counting on you, so don't blow it or you'll pay for it."

As he drove off, I remember thinking, "Wow, this is pretty serious stuff to put in the hands of a teenager…hundreds of thousands of dollars on the line…I'd better come through on this or they may dock my pay for the rest of my life."

Then there's the responsibility that has come from leading a church for over three decades. The responsibility to see that a congregation of hundreds of people is well led, fed, and headed in the right direction. The responsibility to see that infants, children, teens, and adults have vital, meaningful and age-appropriate ministries. The responsibility to see that hundreds of volunteer positions are filled with trained, equipped, and inspired personnel. The responsibility to see that finances are raised and stewarded very wisely. The responsibility to see that paid staff are hired and then fruitful and fulfilled.

There are other responsibilities I carry in life, as well, but none weigh heavier on me than the responsibility I feel for you four children whom God has entrusted to me. Long before I became a dad, I knew that the way I would deal with my children, the way I would interact with, respond to, speak to, and parent would go a long, long way to shaping them and would have a powerful influence in determining the kind of people they would become. The values they would build their lives on, how they would view themselves, and what they would do with their lives all would be impacted by my parenting. And I was so right in this assessment.

It is a responsibility so heavy that at times I almost stagger under the weight of it and it has been the cause of a few late night "cry out to God, ceiling staring" sessions.

The hopes, dreams, and parenting efforts of Mom and me have been fourfold:

1. For you to know you have a heavenly Father and an earthly father and mother who are head over heels in love with you.

2. For you to grow to be a whole, well-adjusted fully devoted follower of Christ.

3. That you will discover, develop, and leverage your God-given strengths and abilities to full potential.

4. That you will have rich, rewarding, and fulfilling relationships.

What loving parent wouldn't want that for their own flesh and blood. And thinking parents understand that hopes and dreams like that don't just magically and mysteriously happen. It calls for real intentionality when so many other things beckon for the best of you. It calls for monster levels of perseverance through the inevitable ups and downs of life and the inevitable push back from the kids themselves. It calls for the very best of your thinking, prayers, and energy.

Once again, personal responsibility comes into play. So, whose job is it to parent our kids in this way? Well, it's the parent's job, right? Parenting cannot be outsourced to teachers, little league, soccer, or cheerleading coaches, nor can it be off-loaded to neighbors, churches, or nannies. Ultimately, the parenting job belongs to the parent. Right? Right!

Parenting to me has been part science, part art, and all prayer. On more that one occasion, I have found myself on my knees praying every parent's prayer: "Oh, God…help! I'm in way over my head!" And the good news is that somehow, some way, through someone or something, God always provided the direction or help.

There are three guiding principles for parenting that Mom and I have followed since day one with you kids and they have served us well. I'm not sure where or how these principles were introduced to us, I simply know we are indebted to our parents and other good parents we have learned from along the way. We know these guiding principles can be trusted and if you follow them, they will not lead you astray in this most important adventure of parenting.

Principle #1: Balance Love and Limits

Okay, as I have already said, parenting is no easy assignment. It calls for the best of our prayers, wisdom, attention, and efforts. The task of taking an utterly dependent infant and growing them up to be a fully independent adult is no lay up. The task of moving someone from childish irresponsibility to responsible maturity is enormous and one key guiding principle in accomplishing this is to balance love and limits.

My sail boat came with some auxiliary power, an outboard motor. The fuel it runs on is a mixture of oil and gas. Too much oil and the engine runs rich; too little and it runs lean, neither are very good for the motor in the long haul. With children, you've got to find the right mixture of love and limits. Love without limits usually leads to a disaster or self-destruction. Limits without love crushes the spirit, extinguishes self-esteem, and often results in rebellion, again neither are very good for the long haul. From my experience, one of the greater parenting challenges has been to find that delicate balance between love and limits, because you kids are all at such different stages of life. With a span of 10 years between first and last, there was a time when Sarah was in high school, Jonathan in middle school, Michael in elementary school, and Bethany was preschool-age. Toss in different temperaments and personalities and you can see how the balance of love and limits had to be handled and adjusted for both stage of life and difference in personality.

First, you've got to have love and lots of it. Early on in this wonderful thing called parenting, I was fortunate enough to have listened to a teacher I greatly respect by the name of Bill Hybels, who wrote a study and gave a talk on this very thing. In fact, much of what I say here is a reflection of what I gleaned from that talk and have sought to follow as a dad.

It's been said that what a child really needs in order to grow up and function optimally as an adult is at least one person who has an irrational involvement in their life. And people who grow to become fairly healthy, well-adjusted adults can almost always look back to at least one parent who loved them irrationally.

When I first heard this, the word irrational hit my ear and raced all the way to the deepest recesses of my head and heart and landed with an echo-producing thud. In other words, I was being told, in order to grow up "normal," a human being has to be loved "abnormally." If a parent really gets and lives this, then a child gets just what their heart needs: love.

Then I learned that the opposite is generally true, as well. People who seem to continually struggle through life, people who do not become well-adjusted adults or fall into extremes, usually are people who cannot recall being loved irrationally by either parent.

It hit me that love is not just a "good thing" for a kid to know and experience, love is not just important, love sounds like it is a make it or break it deal. No parent gets this perfect, but thankfully, God's amazing love can fill in where human love is inadequate. However, every parent should find a way to clearly communicate to the deepest levels of the soul, so a child knows they are prized and cherished. They should grow up in an environment where the experience of love seems as normal as breathing. Their efforts recognized. Their accomplishments celebrated. Their stories worth stopping for and really listening to. Their hopes and dreams believed in. Their activities worth being a lock on your schedule. Their soul worth hearing tens of thousands of times that they are loved by a dad and mom who are head over heels crazy about them.

Now, lest we forget, lest we drift off into a haze of sentimentality, we must remember that rearing these little bundles of love calls for balance. The reality is, children have a streak of something in them that will make parenting an intense character-building challenge. The whole parenting drama has stretched me to the edge of human wisdom and beyond. As a parent, you are going to have to set limits for your kids. Sooner or later, they will demonstrate defiant attitudes, selfish actions, disobedient behaviors, smart mouths, and any number of other unacceptable behaviors.

If you let these sort of things go unchecked, they grow and expand until eventually things can get out of control. These sort of things can ship wreck their lives and do damage to others, as well. If we let our kids grow up without limits, boundaries, consequences, responsibility, and accountability, we are just about guaranteeing them a lifetime of heartache and disaster.

So, it means setting limits on what and how long. Limits on what they watch on TV, movies they see, Internet sites they visit, the way they speak, what they wear, what time they come in, and so on. There will come times when you will also set limits on the friends they associate with. Scripture is so spot on when it says bad company corrupts good character. There will come a time...somewhere in your child's teen years and early twenties where your influence will wane and the influence of the kids they associate with will surge. So, early on teach the kids to choose good friends and early on steer them away from close relationships with kids whose influence is not in line with the values important to you. Then be really street smart as they mature, stay dialed into who they spend time with, the environments they are a part of and be the parent...remember that's your job, be the parent.

Solomon once said, "A rod and a reprimand impart wisdom, but children left to themselves disgrace their mother." Proverbs 29:15.

Discipline can take many forms. A good talking to, time-outs, restrictions, loss of rewards, the occasional "controlled and not in anger" spanking, or natural consequences are some options. (We reserved a swat on the hind side for deliberate defiance.) Often natural consequences where there will be no life-long penalty to pay can be quite the teacher. Not all children respond to the same form of discipline and some "limit infractions" call for different degrees and forms of discipline. And obviously, forms of discipline change as the child grows, so be wise. You've got to find out what works with each child, but as a reminder, don't discipline when you are on the edge of losing control of yourself. Oh, and of course, the kids at times will howl at what an "unfair, fascist dictator" you are. And they will let you know, in no uncertain terms, that they are the only child alive, on the face of this earth with these limitations. (Aww the memories.) But…some time later, they grow up, leave home, and the day comes when they thank you for it.

Your mom and I love, absolutely love, being your parents. But we will be the first to admit, at times, we felt we were in over our heads and all we could do was pray the parents prayer: "Oh, God…help!" Balancing love and limits can be a real challenge.

When do you say, "Kids will be kids…" and give them slack? And when do you say that behavior or attitude crosses the line? When do we intervene in our children's decision-making process in order to protect them and when do we stand back and let them learn the hard lessons of life? When do we comfort tenderly and when do we confront forcefully? When do we encourage and when do we admonish? When do we speak up and correct? When do we stay quiet and listen?

So, we often cried out, "Oh, God… help!" and He always seemed to provide the direction and guidance we needed. Sometimes through Scripture, sometimes through books, friends, or counselors…but He always provides help.

Balance love and limits. Love irrationally. Discipline carefully.

Principle #2: Give Them a Keel and Sails

Sailboats come with two very important and essential components: a keel and sails. The keel is attached to the bottom of the sailboat and is a necessary counter balance to keep the boat from sliding sideways across the surface of the water as the wind blows. It also helps keep the boat upright when stormy wind and waves toss you around like a cork in a Jacuzzi. Sails are used to catch the wind and create movement. Sails and a keel, both are necessary if you are going to sail.

Children need the same. A keel heavy enough to keep them from sliding off course with every little new wind of ideology or culture that blows along and heavy enough to keep them upright in the storms of life. Then they need sails. Sails that will move them through life and allow them to reach their full potential.

First, kids need a keel. As much as we may wish we could shelter and protect our kids from all the pain, difficulties, and set backs of life… it's just not how life works, is it? Life doesn't always go as planned. Our kids will take emotional, relational, financial hits in this life. They will know disappointments, heartaches, and dead end streets because life can just beat you up at times, can't it?

Rather than your child's life falling apart, running aground, going turtle, or sinking, they need a keel to keep them upright. That keel is a spiritual one. It is a relationship with God through faith in Jesus Christ.

Solomon once said, "Those who fear the Lord have a secure fortress, and for their children it will be a refuge." Proverbs 14:26. We can give our kids this spiritual keel by teaching them to build their lives on the Lord and doing the same ourselves. It means every week putting them in a spiritually enriched environment where they learn how to know, walk with, and serve the Lord, so they can be vitally connected to the God of heaven who heals broken hearts, restores dreams, provides direction, makes a way when there is no way, revives weary spirits, is a refuge, gives all the strength needed to make it through the day, offers a reason to go on, and brings so much love, purpose, and meaning to our lives.

As a parent, I realize I can only do so much and the rest is up to you and God. I feel secure knowing God will do His part. As a parent, it means doing my part and putting my kids in the right environment.

One of the best gifts my parents gave me was a spiritual keel, a relationship with God through faith in Jesus Christ. It has kept me upright through the worst storms of life that I've had to face. It has kept me from being blown off course through times of doubt and uncertainty. My parents did their best to put my sister and me in spiritually enriched environments and it has paid off in spades in both our lives. I fear to think where I would be and what my life would be like if it were not for this keel.

Kids also need sails—crisp, well maintained, and positioned sails. These sails are raised to optimally catch the wind and head into a preferred future. This involves decisions, usually an ongoing series of decisions about how much sail should be raised and what is the best position for the sails to be in to best catch the wind. Decisions, decisions, decisions. Correct sail decisions will increase boat speed and make the ride smoother. Wrong sail decisions can lead to the rough ride of being overpowered or the opposite when you feel like you are pulling a plow along the briny bottom. Sail size, shape, and position can be critical decisions.

The same is true for our kids. Not just the decisions we make on their behalf, but also the kind of decision makers we help our kids to become. Life really is a series of decisions, isn't it? From the mundane, like what color shirt should I wear to huge life-shaping decisions like where do I live and whom do I marry. There are a thousand other decisions in between about morality, entertainment, sexuality, finances, and on and on. Life is a series of decisions. If you can teach your kids to be wise decision-makers, you can greatly increase the likelihood that they will lead a significant and successful life. Fail to raise up good decision-makers, and you can just about count on your children experiencing more than their share of mistakes, heartaches, regrets, missed opportunities, and the payment of "stupid-tax."

Solomon said it like this: "Start children off on the way they should go, and even when they are old they will not turn from it." Proverbs 22:6. As a general rule, this Proverb says the pattern we set for our children during their early years will eventually take root in their lives and those patterns will become their own. So, if we deliberately and diligently model and teach good decision-making, eventually our kids will do the same for themselves. And remember, kids face a ton of pressure in their lives to go down the wrong paths. These may be paths that perhaps their peers are encouraging them to go down, so they fit in and don't stand out as weird. Paths that the media and entertainment industry suggest is normal and expected, but paths you may not want your child traveling down. The day comes when you will not be present to make or influence these decisions on their behalf and your child will have to decide for himself or herself. If they are not equipped to make good decisions at that moment...look out.

This business of I'll just let my son or daughter go through life experiencing things for themselves and decide on their own which path they should take, is not a well thought through approach to parenting.

It may sound enlightened, but it sure breaks down in application. The reality is that in taking this approach all you are doing is deciding you won't be the one influencing your child's decision-making process. You are simply surrendering that influence to what they see on TV, movies, or the Internet; surrendering that influence to what they hear at school from their peers or in musical lyrics.

Solomon says teach your children to make good decisions. How? Well, here are a few ideas to help in that regard:

- You model good decision making for your kids. When you make a good decision, tell the kids how you nailed it. When you miss, be honest, tell them how and where you blew it and what you learned.

- Utilize the crucible of life. When you see people choosing the wrong path or making poor decisions on TV, the news or in life, point it out to the kids. When you see the opposite and you see people choosing the right path, affirm it.

- Teach them to do their homework. Gather data, information, and do research. What do you need to know to make a great decision?

- Ask the experts. Who are the people you respect, who make better decisions than you? Ask them personally, read their books, listen to their teachings…ask yourself "What would _____ do?"

- Use your values as a guideline. Does the decision honor the core values of what you believe to be true? Yes or no.

- Visit the depository of pain. Pain is a fantastic teacher. Keep a "pain file" from bad past decisions, so you can remind yourself that you have paid the "pain piper" enough. Better yet, borrow scar tissue and learn from the pain of others.

- Listen for the promptings of the Holy Spirit of God. The wisdom of God sometimes defies conventional wisdom and God promises to share it liberally with His children. So ask for and listen to the promptings and leadings of God. Assign one ear to heaven as you go through your day and listen for the still, small voice of God.

Principle #3: Keep it Simple and Strategic

I've watched parents fret and stew trying to give their kid every opportunity and every advantage to the point of over-enrolling them in every activity under the sun and in the process stress out themselves and their kids trying to be and do everything. The result is one very stressed out life and home. Here are a few simple guidelines.

Repeat the mantra: "This, too, shall pass."

Your kids will go through all kinds of phases, stages, and transitions. At times you will feel tried to your wits ends… and you will be. You will wonder will it always be like this…the answer is "no." So hang on, pray, lean into others. It will not always be like this. This, too, shall pass.

Be fully present.

The day will come when the kids will leave the house for good and be off on their own. Some days it may seem like that day will never get here. It does get here and much faster than you realize. Time is relative. The day will come when you realize that days passed slowly, but the years flew by. So, treasure the moments. Put down the paper. Turn off the TV or computer and look your child in the eye and really listen. Let them know that what is important to them is important to you, because they are important to you. What matters to them, matters to you, because they matter to you. Arrange your schedule to be present at games, recitals, school open houses, parties, and meal times. You cannot recapture nor recreate missed moments. New ones can be made and captured, but yesterdays moments are gone, so be present today.

Don't make mountains out of mole hills.

Keep things in perspective, especially when you are tired, over-extended, or stressed. A carpet stained by juice can either be cleaned or replaced; a soul stained by angry, degrading words—not so easy to recover. Dented cars can be fixed; a dinged self-esteem—not so easily repaired. Things are things and things burn in the end, but your child is of infinite value. So, when you overreact, over discipline, or over speak…it's okay and recommended that parents acknowledge such and apologize. Your kids will respect you for it.

Keep your word.

When you make a promise to your child…keep your promise. Say you'll be there…be there. Tell them something will happen, big or little…make it happen. Your credibility shapes their dependability.

Establish meaningful traditions.

Traditions give your kids a sense of stability, roots, and confidence in a few things that they can count on. Maybe it's birthday or Christmas traditions, it could be vacation, post-doctor visit, or Sunday traditions, but give them a few things in this ever-changing world that is a sure bet.

Don't forget to have fun.

Every now and then, do things the kids enjoy doing. Maybe it doesn't necessarily float your boat, but it does theirs. Make sure you join in and do it. When you do things that are fun together…it makes it fun to be together.

As you go through life, people will measure you by a variety of metrics. How many square feet comprised your home? What was your job title? What kind of salary did you pull down? What kind of cars did you drive? Whose name was on your designer clothes? Where did you vacation? And there will be days, if not seasons, when you find yourself giving your best to go up and to the right on those charts. It's all nice, but the day comes when you realize that what matters infinitely more is what kind of a dad or what kind of a mom you are and what kind of a relationship you have with those kids God has entrusted to you? Not that you can't have it all, but if you must choose between being the dad or mom the kids need you to be or climbing the next rung on the career ladder...kids win. The day comes when you will find greater joy and fulfillment in the accomplishments of your kids than you do in your own. The sooner that day comes for you, the better for both you and your kids.

I have been called many things in my life: pastor, boss, leader, neighbor, coach, sailor, and a few other mentionable and unmentionable names, but the one that means the most by a country mile is Dad. May you have children who bring you as much joy as you have brought me. I absolutely love being your dad.

www.ingramcontent.com/pod-product-compliance
Lightning Source LLC
LaVergne TN
LVHW091202080426
835509LV00006B/786